WITHDRAWN

The Mirror Dance

The Mirror Dance

IDENTITY IN A WOMEN'S COMMUNITY

Susan Krieger

TEMPLE UNIVERSITY PRESS
Philadelphia

Temple University Press, Philadelphia 19122
© 1983 by Susan Krieger. All rights reserved
Published 1983
Printed in the United States of America

Library of Congress Cataloging in Publication Data

Krieger, Susan.
   The mirror dance.

      1. Lesbians—Middle West—Psychology.   2. Community
life—Psychological aspects.   3. Identity (Psychology)
4. Intimacy (Psychology)   5. Separation (Psychology)
6. Stigma (Social psychology)   I. Title.
HQ75.6.U5K73   1983   306.7′663′0977   82-19424
ISBN 0-87722-304-1

For our communities

Contents

Contents

Preface

In the late 1970s, while spending a year as a visiting assistant professor at a university in a midwestern town, I participated as a member of a lesbian community in that town. At the end of my stay I conducted the seventy-eight interviews on which this study is based. When I left the community the following summer for a job elsewhere, I took with me four hundred pages of single-spaced typed interview notes, a collection of journals and stories I had written about my experience in the community, a collection of community newsletters, bits and pieces of correspondence, a blue shirt and a book of good wishes that were going-away gifts from community members, and many important personal allegiances and memories.

During the next two years, I found that it was not a simple matter to move from my experience of intimate involvement with the community to a sociological analysis of that experience. I spent a year alternately picking up and putting down my interview notes before I learned that, in order to progress, I had to confront the ambivalence of my personal feelings toward the community in which I had lived and done my research. The process of exploring my own experience led me ultimately to see that feelings similar to my own were important in the accounts of the women I had interviewed and enabled me to use those feelings to guide my larger analysis. That analysis resulted in

Preface

The Mirror Dance, a study that focuses on problems of merger and separation and on conflicts surrounding identity.

Many people helped me with this work. I am indebted, first of all, to the women of the community whose experiences form the heart of this book. I want to thank them, although I cannot name them, for cooperating with my research, for taking me in when I was a stranger, and for struggling with the difficult problems this study describes.

I am indebted to other friends and colleagues as well. I want to thank Marythelma Brainard, who helped me with ideas about interpersonal boundaries, merger, and separation and also helped me grow, and Cleo Eulau who, earlier, taught me much about separation. Fourteen years ago, Peter Marris modeled being a sociologist for me and the spirit of his work has been behind mine ever since. James G. March repeatedly let me know that he felt I was worthwhile and that he would read with pleasure anything I wrote. Ann Swidler read, reread, and talked with me about self-other and self-community relationships, sharing her magic for understanding. Martin H. Krieger was, as always, a source of unconditional support. At crucial times, Rita J. Simon also gave me much-needed acceptance and support. Estelle Freedman helped me decide to write up this study when I was uncertain and then encouraged me to deal with its hardest problems. Her insights, her suggestions, and her caring have enriched each of its drafts. In addition, there are other friends who, over the years, have talked with me and shared experiences similar to those reflected in this book. I want to thank them for their knowledge and for their love. *The Mirror Dance* is about a particular community; it is also, more broadly, about us all.

Introduction

This book is about individual identity in a women's community. It is based on a year of participant-observation that culminated in two months of intensive interviewing with seventy-eight women who were either members of the community or importantly associated with it. The community—a loose-knit social group composed primarily of lesbians—was located in a midwestern town and had approximately sixty active members.

When I spoke with the women of this community, I initially intended to study privacy. I asked four basic questions: (1) How would you define privacy (what images come to mind)? (2) How would you define the local lesbian community? (3) Within that community, how have you been concerned about boundaries between public and private, self and other (i.e., what has been your personal and social history)? (4) With respect to the outside world, how have you been concerned about protecting the fact of your lesbianism (who knows, who does not, and why)?

In time, however, I came to understand that my inquiries into privacy required me to explore dilemmas of identity. I moved from thinking of privacy as an ability to close the door of a house in order to protect oneself from view, to thinking that, more accurately, it was an ability to both open and close the door to affect how one might be known. I came, in other words, to be concerned about control over definition of the self. I also came to realize that my study was destined to be about something even more compelling to me: the problem of loss of sense of self—how it occurs and how it may be dealt with in a social setting.

The community I had studied, it seemed to me, presented a basic identity conflict to members and potential members. On the one hand, it promised them that, within it, they would be affirmed for who they truly and fully were. Here they might find haven from the outside world, acceptance not available elsewhere, and confirmation of crucial feelings they had about themselves, feelings related to their lesbianism, their feminism, and their identification as women. On the other hand, in this community, they would often feel that their differences from others were not valued, their own unique identities given little recognition or room. The community, in other words, would often seem to threaten their sense of selfhood.

This, I came to feel, was true in large part because the community was a community of likeness, one in which individuals were encouraged to value a common identity as women. It was also a community of intimacy in which members were given support for experiences of closeness and union, including those which might reach their peak in shared sexuality. It was a community of ideology and, in particular, of an ideology that stressed the oneness of women working together for a better life, an ideology that dealt minimally, if at all, with possibilities for conflict latent in the differences between members. It was a stigmatized or deviant community, a condition that also emphasized the need for oneness and solidarity. It was a relatively new community and so lacked many predetermined rules and roles that might give its members established ways of exercising their differences. Finally, and not of the least consequence, it was a community of women: individuals with life experiences that tended to encourage, indeed to view as virtuous, the giving up of the self to others.

Individuals faced with the reality of such a group were especially likely, it seemed to me, to experience a threat to their sense of personal boundary, individuality, or separate self. This threat would not always be felt by all people, but it would be felt by many on occasion, perhaps by all at some time, and by some to a greater degree than others. Particular situations or relationships within the community might bring it out. The individual would then experience a sense of loss of self or loss of control over her identity as a complete and separate person. In the words of one of my interviewees, she would cease to be "anything that was clear to her."

This experience of loss of a sense of self would characteristically take two forms. (1) The individual might feel overwhelmed: she might have a sense of losing herself to the community or some part of it by being taken over, subordinated, in effect suffocated by it; she might feel she was being given little room for herself, little time or space to respond to her own needs; she might feel too entangled with the community, too caught up in its pattern of inbred relationships, too defined by the group and its norms rather than by her own. Or, (2) the individual might feel abandoned by the community and experience a sense of loss of self when it seemed that the group or some part of it had left her, rejected her, or failed to fulfill her expectations that it would be a supportive, nurturing, or caring environment. She might then feel isolated within the group, starved, left out, disappointed; she might feel generally that the group was not there for her, not truly responsive to her.

Individuals might be in one or the other of these emotional positions (feeling overwhelmed or abandoned) at different times; they might alternate between them; or they might feel them simultaneously. Certain individuals might tend to have more experiences in one position than the other. They might often, in anticipation of an experience of one or the other kind, take steps to avoid it. Their experiences and their responses to them might, in fact, reflect basic expectations of being overwhelmed or abandoned that they had prior to coming to the community. But the important thing is that whatever the prior histories of individuals, the community brought out such experiences frequently, and often in extreme form, over a wide variety of cases. It did so by offering, on the one hand, a strong promise of identity affirmation stemming from what its members had in common and, on the other, a lack of established mechanisms for dealing with the differences between members.

At the same time, however, the community seemed to push both members and others toward finding new ways of protecting and defining their sense of self. Very often the experience of loss of a sense of identity was, despite its difficulty, seized upon as an opportunity for identity clarification. Such clarification would result from processes in which individuals would come and go in relation to the community, comparing, contrasting, and developing ideas of themselves in relation to others as they did so. Clarification also came from processes in which an individual would learn to structure her relationships within the community in ways that made the terms of those relationships explicit, reliable, and responsive to her needs. By structuring her relationships both with the community as a whole and with its members, the individual could, it seemed, emerge from experiences of loss of a sense of self with resources for dealing with the distressing feelings of being overwhelmed or abandoned. She would have a better sense of boundaries between herself and others and, as a result, she would be more aware of herself as a complete and separate person.

Yet the experience leading to such an end would often be highly conflictual and, indeed, painful. The individual attempts to be part of the community, to be like others in the group, to merge symbiotically; simultaneously, she seeks a sense of herself through processes of separating, being different, being an individual distinct from the group. In her efforts to join with the group, she runs the risk of being overwhelmed. In her efforts to be separate, she runs the risk of abandonment. She is caught, sometimes painfully, between the two risks in a conflict between needs for likeness and for difference and the support each lends identity. Only sometimes, however, and often after the fact, does she realize that this conflict may be part of a process in which she learns about herself and in which, by structuring her relationships with others, she develops a clearer and perhaps better conception of who she is, sometimes seemingly in opposition to the group, at other times in conjunction with it.

Now all social groups—communities, organizations, families—confront their members with this kind of conflict. In all groups there is a tension between the individual's desire to be part of a whole and the desire to be different. In all groups there are risks of being overwhelmed or abandoned, and individuals faced with these risks may at times experience a loss of sense of self, or loss of control over identity. Yet in some groups this experience is felt more intensely than in others and seems to occur more frequently. In some groups the expected negative consequences of taking either risk seem greater and, at the same time, the identity clarification that may result is more needed.

In those groups where the desire for personal affirmation from the group is great, and the complementary desire for assertion of individuality is also strong, the conflict between likeness and difference may be unusually acute. In these groups, the dilemmas produced by such a conflict are seen especially clearly, with a good deal of their complexity apparent. A lesbian community is such a group. Examining it may be particularly instructive for understanding how a sense of loss of self, or loss of control over identity, may be related to a larger socially structured conflict and how such a conflict may be mediated in any social setting.

Within a lesbian community, we find that individuals constantly have to deal with the mirror images they present to each other and with the difficulty of developing a sense of self-identity that is different from the common identity that their group encourages. In this type of group, members must repeatedly improvise solutions which structure their relationships with one another so that they can emerge from experiences of loss of sense of self with an identity that is different from the identity of others who look very much like them. Because of the

nature of this effort, and because it suggests the basic struggle
with likeness that lies at the heart of the community's reality, I
have titled this book *The Mirror Dance.* The phrase was used by
one of the women I interviewed in speaking of the difficulties of
couple relationships in the community, the place where, because intimacy is so highly valued and possibilities for merger
are great, problems of loss of sense of self are felt most acutely.

To best portray these problems, *The Mirror Dance* has been
organized in three parts. Part I provides an overview of the
nature of the community and the ways individuals perceive it as
structuring identity dilemmas for them. It also suggests how
individuals characteristically respond to those dilemmas. Part II
examines particular kinds of situations and relationships within
the community where conflicts concerning control over identity
are especially prominent. Finally, Part III steps outside the community and attempts to gain perspective by looking back at it.
The chapters of the book may be read in any order, but the sense
of the whole they convey is one that builds in the sequence in
which they appear.

As will be evident, the book as a whole is written in an
unusual manner. It describes and explains its community's
dilemmas exclusively through the voices of community members. The book reads rather like a novel in that it proceeds by
association, by ordering the stories of many different individuals to create a sense of a whole. Its analysis emerges through
its ordering: in the way it juxtaposes, compares, and connects
the different viewpoints it represents. It encourages the reader to
grasp that analysis by identifying with the book's characters and
the experiences they discuss. The result of this process should
be an increasing familiarity with patterns that are pervasive and
repetitive in the community, and that structure identity problems for members, but which are not well summarized in terms
of abstract concepts. Rather, the methodological contention of
this work is that here, as elsewhere in social science, pattern
may be best represented through description. (This point is
discussed further in the book's Appendix.)

The Mirror Dance is clearly an experiment, both in women's language and in social science method.* It is composed of an interplay of voices that echo, again and again, themes of self and community, sameness and difference, merger and separation, loss and change. Speaking in the colloquial style of the community, these voices provide their own narration. There is no authorial voice in the body of the work, except in the first chapter which is designed to set the scene. In the remaining chapters, the voices of community members alone analyze and comment upon one another and guide the reader to an appreciation of the conflicts surrounding identity in the community. The reader may find that, at times, the voices of these women merge with one another and become indistinguishable; individuals with different names speak as if they were one, reflecting the extent to which the community is a community of likeness. At other times, the same persons stand out from others as separate and different, and are therefore more easily identifiable. In this way, the text illustrates its own thesis: that clarity about identity occurs through push-and-pull processes as individuals join and draw back; respond to loss and confusion; feel, on the one hand, dependence on community and, on the other, apartness from it.

The Mirror Dance is thus both document and analysis. It is built on the interpretation this Introduction sets forth and yet it is open to other interpretations. It invites the reader to join, to take part, to overhear the gossip of women in one particular subcommunity in a midwestern town, to come to know the members of this community, to share their insights and their confusions. The challenge is to adopt these women temporarily as a peer group, to muddle through their difficulties with them, and to confront one's own responses to those difficulties as they appear when articulated through the book's interplay of many voices.

*For a review of more traditional social science approaches to the study of lesbian identity and community, see Susan Krieger "Lesbian Identity and Community: Recent Social Science Literature," *Signs*, vol 8, no. 1 (Autumn 1982).

Introduction

The picture of the community that appears in this study is not intended to be objective; nor is it arbitrary. It is a structured representation of a particular problem, loss of sense of self; in a particular setting, a women's community; and of possibilities for achieving clarity about individual identity in circumstances of stress. My hope is that the insights and the sense of reality this study offers may be of use to individuals who must deal with problems similar to those of the women whose experience it describes. These, most especially, will be lesbians—those who are not members of self-defined subcommunities no less importantly than those who are. I would also like this work to be of use to others whose identity dilemmas are similar. Perhaps most crucially, I would like it to provide a sociological perspective on individual difficulty and to contribute to the development of that body of studies within sociology that represents abstract social processes in concrete organizational and subgroup settings.

The Mirror Dance

PART I

1

The Setting

It was a medium-sized midwestern town. The trees were large, the landscape flat, the houses set apart, each fronted with a plot of green. In the winter it was covered with snow. In the summer the air was thick with humidity and the streets were overarched with splendid heavy branches. One could walk across town in an hour and a half, drive across in less than fifteen minutes. The winters were long and people complained of cabin fever as they wore on.

It was a town in the middle of America. Bus service stopped before midnight and ceased entirely on Sundays after 4:00 P.M. Just beyond the city limits on all sides were fields of corn. On Saturdays men mowed lawns during those months when lawns mattered. In the winter cars skidded on ice and quite often the airport closed down, as did the highways, producing an isolation that felt complete. A few miles in any direction were smaller farming towns whose residents didn't place much stock in the university "in town," although maybe their children attended the community college. There was one main shopping center out north, and the downtown, renewed and paved with red brick, saw little use. It was a good place to raise children. The neighborhoods, with the exclusion of the south central area, were fairly safe. The bus stops were well lit. There were a few parks within the city limits and a larger one just outside, and many of the streets were cobblestoned.

The Mirror Dance

It was a town where people had families, a town where the bars were not, among the majority white population, a place to go, a town where it was hard to get a foreign car fixed, impossible to get a French meal and nearly as hard to find good Chinese, a town of fast pizza and big crowds at the K-Mart and on the 4th of July. One could get by without reading the local paper or listening to the local news, though people for the most part did not. Events of the larger outside world only sometimes impinged, as if the cornfields and the long straight roads and the fragile airport that were the town's connections to anywhere in fact functioned in reverse.

It was a gray place beneath a gray sky, most of it paved in gray, especially near the cement factory. People grew strong here. They valued being settled; they valued the fact that they were in the Midwest, America's heartland where the real people lived, not crazy people like they had in California or caught up with themselves like in New York. If the Russians bombed, it was safe to assume they would probably never drop anything near; or it used to be safe to assume that before students and a few professors from the university started telling people different. It was a town where you either came and went quickly or you stayed for a long time.

Once a month on a Friday night, a group of women would gather upstairs in a church not far from the center of town and meet and talk about what it was like to live here and to feel different—to feel part of a separate community. There would be between twenty and forty of them wandering in over several hours' time. They would bring wine and punch and, of course, there was coffee, for this meeting was what they called a coffee-house. They had been getting together this way for several years, beginning when there were only five or ten of them. They'd wear slacks and overalls, and in the winter they'd pile a table high with bulky jackets. The heat would sometimes be on, sometimes not. The room was large and wood-panelled and it had a fireplace. Space in it sometimes would be cleared away and the women would dance.

Other times they'd just sit around in a big circle and talk about their sense of community: who they thought they were, what they were trying to do, how they wanted as a group to "be there" for each other, to lend tools, to feel support, to be able to share their lives as they might not on their jobs or at school or with the families from which they came. Occasionally a few of them would talk about going out to speak to classes and to other groups to tell people how they were really quite like others in the town. Their homes were the homes of your neighbors, their way of life really not as strange as it seemed.

Newcomers would frequently first enter the community these women formed by coming to their coffeehouse meetings, having found out about them from an ad in the university paper, an annoucement in the community newsletter, or by word of mouth, and often they would be shy, wondering if this was a group they really wanted to be part of. If they stayed, most likely they'd be invited to come to the bar after, or to come some other time to one of the women's houses for a party or to have dinner. In spring or summer, if they lasted through the winter, they might come, as well, to a picnic or a special celebration held in one of the local parks. They might join a ball team or one of the small support groups that met each week; they might sing in the choir.

There were about sixty women actively involved in this group which called itself "the community," though the number you'd usually see together at any one time was more likely to be around twenty-five, and there were others beyond the sixty who took part but only occasionally. These women ranged in age from eighteen to fifty-one with the majority in their mid-twenties or early thirties. They were for the most part lesbian, some were feminists, a few simply woman-identified. They were white and middle class and most of them at some time or another had connection with the community college or the university. They were students, teachers, administrators, nurses, production workers, jewelers, waitresses, and printers. They were not a communal group, though they sought to de-

5

velop those possibilities. They lived in separate houses: some together as couples, some in cooperative homes, many alone. A few came in from outlying towns where maybe they lived in a big, old farmhouse. Several had kids.

They joined the community looking for something and sometimes thinking they'd found it. When she had finally found these people, said one of the women, she felt she had finally found people who would accept her whole life and she didn't want to let them go. The community for her, said another, was a group of women she could know she could lean on for support or just let her hair down around. It was a group of women who allowed circumstances and places where she could be herself.

Yet often the hopes for being oneself here met with disappointment: "You would think it would be easier to assert your differences in a community of women," said Irene, "but it's not. It's real disillusioning." Or, "It gets down to the crucial thing that everybody's complaining about," said Carol, "which is not being able to be themselves. It's not that everybody has to approve of me, but I want to be accepted."

The community seemed to offer a promise: "Here are women who can understand me, touch me the way I want to be touched," Melissa felt. At the same time it provided an experience which was disconcerting: "In the process of all that happened, all that mutual discovery of pleasure within our community, I think I lost a sense of my own development separate from other people."

2

An Identity Community

She saw several different lesbian communities in town, said Ruth, though she understood what people meant when they said "the community." It was definitely the most out, the most woman-identified. It was a group of women who were almost exclusively lesbians, who had been out or around for just about as long as she had been here, which was about five years, or longer than that. These were women who were the lesbian community almost because it was important to them and because they found a sense of being, belonging, fellowship, and sharing that way.

By and large, they had known each other for a number of years, many of them, or at least the nucleus; they were people who had chosen to remain here. They were mostly older than student age, professionals, people who had life ties here, and if they were students, they were graduate students. That was basically the core of the group that was meant as the lesbian community. As a claim to being "the community" they probably had it, she thought, because they named themselves in such a way and wanted it.

They were a real tight-closed group, felt Norah, a group that was closed until they knew for sure that you were a lesbian for one thing. And she didn't think that you could just go meet them, go hang out with them. She thought you had to join them, which happened if you knew somebody.

They were basically a social network, felt Irene. The common denominator was people who defined themselves as lesbians. The community was a social entity that had its own rules, its own membership, its own qualifications. It was primarily devoted to itself rather than a proselytizing organization (like a church or Rape Crisis). It had functions: it gave its members a group identity; it gave them support for their life style and a sense of security and affirmation; for some people who didn't have a strong identity other than the fact of their lesbianism, it was crucial. It was also exclusive. The membership qualifications were pretty narrowly defined: a woman had to be either sexually involved with another woman, or planned to be, or had a good strong history of having been.

But more than that was that the most important thing in 85 percent of the cases was a person's affectional life, or the way a person dealt with her relationships with other people. It focused, the community focused, Irene felt, on how somebody was in relation to somebody else. It had a lot to do with the other and how the individual developed herself in an abstract sense: how she developed in terms of ideas she had about herself in relation to others.

The community consisted, said Valerie, of a loose federation of support groups and the women's service organizations that were linked to these groups (the Women's Shelter, The Rape Crisis Center, the Women's Information Network), plus activity groups like the choir and the sports teams and the newsletter. Then there were women who were not in any of these groups but who related to people who were as friends or lovers and participated in community events: the coffeehouse, the parties, the Seder, the May Day, and Sapphic Plains Collective events like the square dance. And then there were the Arts Festival Collective people.

It didn't seem to be just any women in the larger community who happened to be lesbian, Bronwyn believed. It was a particular group of women who were lesbians and a few who were not, a group of women whose lives touched, who came in contact socially and emotionally.

It was basically women who chose to relate to other women sexually, felt Madeleine, who generally were in relationships with other women, although some were not. But it was the idea of community as opposed to single women relating sexually. There was a whole culture, a camaraderie, a support system, a network, shared understanding, shared vision. Then within that there were strong friendships and people who met each other in cluster arrangements.

They were, felt Lillian—the group that she had observed—many of them were "Ain't it awful." Everybody kept dumping on them. She saw many sick people. It was like you gained your support and identity by putting yourself in a bunch of people who were equally oppressed. She had chosen not to actively identify with them.

It was women who identified as lesbians and feminists so that they had a consciousness of wanting to be part of a community, felt Carol. She thought there had to be an idea of wanting a community for it to exist. Then that was built on by the shared activities, the newsletter, the coffeehouses. She wasn't sure, but she thought there were maybe fifty to a hundred people in it on different levels: a core group and those who were more peripheral.

Right now the lesbian community for her, said Jill, was the potential for being what she would call home.

She came to it six years ago through the Women's Shelter support group, recalled Gayle. That was how the so-called elite group in the community got started. The people in that group all met each other through working on forming the Women's Shelter. Being thirty years old before you met another lesbian, that was where she was then. Going to the Women's Shelter and meeting all these lesbians and finding people saying all these daring radical statements, she just felt her whole life had come together. It was Melissa and Elinor. They were the core of it for her. The daring radical statements ranged from Elinor sitting on the kitchen table doing self-examination, to daring to say the word "lesbian" out loud, to doing a demonstration in support of a woman who didn't wear a bra. It was like she had spent her whole life looking for this one little living room of people arguing.

She was around then too, recalled Ruby, and for her the community was people who identified themselves as lesbians or women-identified women. They came to events of a social nature, maybe sponsored by one of the support groups, some kind of activity that was larger than just friends, and they had some commitment to helping women in a social service sense; so they worked at the Women's Shelter, or babysat for a lesbian mother, or wrote about women. They also usually would talk about the community and not be terribly uncomfortable about not being able to define it.

The community itself, she felt, was changing all the time. It already had gone through several stages. There was a time when it hadn't been as solidified as now, so going outside it wasn't an issue. But now there was much more available. You had all these choices: there was a party every weekend at least, you could have musical activity, you could have sports activity, you could dance at the bar, you could play pool at the bar, you could have religious services, you could carry out your politics with your friends, you could have your job with your friends, you could make love with your friends, you could die with them, everything.

Most of the women she saw were twenty to thirty-five; they had some education beyond high school, were heavily academic for the most part, were middle class and real interested, probably, in exploring the relationship between who they were and the roles they had been playing. That was the larger community in which there were, she would say, about fifty.

Within it there were smaller communities: women who had agency bonds like Rape Crisis or the Women's Shelter; women who had the bond of planning to spend their lives here, who were trying to organize a community in part so it would be there when they were old for survival reasons. Then there was another group that was made up of people who were going to school and wanted to identify with a lesbian community while they were in school, but they were transients. There were also a lot of people who just dropped in and out, like they only came to choir and you never saw them anywhere else. Or they only came to Chip and Jessica's parties. They probably didn't have enough bonds to enough people or groups to make it worth their while to come more often.

These women were the majority community in terms of race, felt Edwina, although their numbers were small. They were predominantly white women; they were growing in ideas and size, so they were a very hungry-minded group of women, a very strong group of women.

They were an anti-intellectual group, said Hollis, very hedonistic, self-interested in that sense of being self-maintaining, very inward-looking. If she wasn't one of them, she didn't think she would find their community admirable. If she didn't need these people socially, she would not have had anything to do with them. What was the community exactly? It was everybody in town she knew, the ones she saw regularly, whose faces were in it. It rested on face-to-face knowledge of one another. She didn't see it as a community really. It was mainly a social network. She thought it was much more a reference group than a community.

Right now, said Nikki, the community she saw was a sexually identified group of women, but she wasn't comfortable with that as a base of much of anything really. It was all women in town who were able to identify a community and include themselves as members. That included some straight women and ruled out some lesbian women who couldn't identify a community, or who could and who didn't want to consider themselves members.

It was mostly very young women, nineteen to thirty, felt Vivian. There seemed to be a broad spectrum of interests. The

11

women tended to be poor. They were much more affectionate, warm or affectionate, than the average acquaintance you might have. They were not necessarily more open or friendly, but they tended to be willing to express their feelings. She kept wishing that everybody in it would get to be about twenty years older, so then she would feel more part of it.

It was a group, said Martha, she had found a few years ago that she really wanted to be part of for the first time in her life. She felt she could count on people here in ways she had never thought of before.

She felt, said Aurora, that this was a group of women who she could call on to have her needs met in whatever way: physical needs or psychological needs, basic needs like moving, a place to sleep if she was having trouble with her own space. It was people who were willing to be open around each other, sharing with each other, sharing feelings.

There were fifteen to twenty women in it, said Pat. These were the most active, the core. They represented no cross section of anything really, which was a problem she had with the whole thing.

There were thirty to forty, she would guess, said Stephanie, an estimate which came from the fact that you usually didn't see more than thirty to forty of the women in one place at one time.

There were a hundred or more, thought Ellen, a number which came from the number of names on the newsletter mailing list. The list had about 140 names on it the last time she mailed it and about a third of them didn't have local addresses.

The number varied, said Maria, depending on how you defined it.

There were other lesbian groups in town, said Ruth, but defining them got tenuous because the farther away you got from this particular group that called itself "the community," the more reluctant women were to name themselves. There was, for example, the P.E. Department at the university. She could probably go through a list of names and tell you who they were, meaning the faculty, and it was funny because they were mostly closeted. Yet everybody knew who was living with who and probably why. "Everybody" was mainly people who were close enough: the P.E. students. They were a kind of community too, They were also fairly closety. There were more than just a few she knew among the students who'd had four or five sexual experiences with women who would nonetheless say they were not gay, who refused the title or the label or even the idea.

There were people in town like Emmy and Priss, felt Alison, who never even went to the bar. They just saw themselves and a couple of other people. They wouldn't be involved in the community. There were people like Nan and Cherry, said Cynthia. Nan drove a truck for UPS. Cherry was from a family of three daughters, two of whom were gay. They lived in a trailer a half-mile down the road. They had a different kind of relationship: a division of labor along traditional male-female lines. Nan worked days. Cherry went to school, high school, and took care of the house. Nan worked funny hours because she drove out in the country. They didn't have a university association or any tie to the community.

There was the trailer park circle, noted Connie, some lesbians who lived in trailers off I-28 northwest of town. There were about six couples out there. They kept mostly to themselves and didn't have to do with the community.

There were the people who lived in the Rose Street house behind where she did, said Norah. You'd see them at the bar. They had their own group. They had identified her with the community, she felt, so they didn't talk to her.

There was this woman in Math, recalled Nell, who parked her car near where she, Nell, did at the university, but who never said anything about it. There was also a dean of something, an old dyke from way back who had short hair and walked tough. Then there were the two women out on McDermid Road who were in Public Health and in their late fifties. Vivian said that if you called them, they'd probably hang up on you. There were probably a lot of people like them who wouldn't have anything to do with the community, who just had six friends.

There were the women at the bar, said Earth, some of whom sometimes came to community events; but mostly they didn't. That was a whole different world. It was the second most visible lesbian community in town.

Then there were those, felt Edwina, who hadn't even come to awareness yet, who going to the bar would be terrifying for, who didn't even know it.

Generally speaking there were "the farm lesbians" who just came in on weekends, noted Judith, as different from "the bar crowd" who used to frequent Leo's all the time, who were just apart from "the intellectual lesbian community." And then there were "the jocks" who could be broken into those who did things with the community and those who had no relationship to it.

She had a lot of trouble, said Millicent, because there were all the lesbians in the area, and then there was a group of people who thought that there was a COMMUNITY. It seemed to her that these people perceived themselves as the be-all and end-all of lesbianism in the four-county area. In ways, they tried to define the lesbian population and make a lesbian feel either part of or not part of the community. These people defined what it was to be a really good lesbian or a really good dyke. For example: you needed to be articulate or aggressive (socially aggressive, party aggressive, like, "Hi, how are you, I have heard about you. Aren't you the one who . . . ?"). You either needed to be a university or a community college person, or a real sincere and hardworking blue collar. If you were from one of the outlying towns, you had a black mark against you in the first place, because you were not likely to be a clever person. For herself, she had been all the way on the inside with them and now she was on the outside.

She was not in the particular group known as the community, said Norah, but she knew them and they knew her. How did she know they knew her? Because they said "Hi" to her on the street. She felt she was probably identified more as Kitty's lover (Kitty was one of them for a while) or Hollis's friend than as herself. But she said "Hi" to them too and she didn't know them.

She mainly knew what she heard from Hollis and Kitty's conversations. From that, from all the gossip, she had decided that she didn't want to get involved with them. She didn't want to be part of an organization. She just didn't think there was any way she could be judged as an individual with that group.

She had gone to one of the Arts Festival concerts last year and looked around for people who had a similar age, education, and socioeconomic level as herself, recalled Lillian, and she had seen a bunch of very overweight, very sloppy, and rather obnoxious people with whom she preferred not to be identified. Opal, her lover, had gone too and Opal thought there were some nice songs in there that talked about life in general, but if there was a line in them about men, it was totally negative. She had problems with that because she considered herself to be a humanist.

She did at times have a yearning to be part of the community, said Opal, but she felt, and she knew by the grapevine, that she would be rejected. She understood that she was seen as snobby. That was based on her occasional appearance at a social gathering where she didn't know anybody well enough to be part of a group so she sat and talked with a few friends and didn't appear for another year; and her involvements were with people who were closety. She was not seen putting up posters.

She had kept a distance from them, said Terry, because she feared an involvement would jeopardize her career and she felt that she simply didn't share that many interests with people in the community.

She hadn't joined, said Joan, because of feeling that she didn't need that kind of group. Also, she didn't buy the line that just being lesbian tied people together.

She came from a poor family, said Leslie. To break into a group that was on the upper level of classism, professionalism, and all that—which was how she saw this community—you needed basically to have confidence in yourself, and she was feeling sometimes, "Only a year of college." But then she thought she had the same skills as any of the others; she just didn't have the categories and the numbers. Finally, by being with these people, by associating with Gloria, she came to feel, "They don't have anything on me."

She first got involved through Aurora, said Roxanne, and she got the feeling that there were certain rules in this community: like you should be a vegetarian and not like red meat or pork and prefer shopping at the natural foods store. These were people who preferred whole wheat bread, wore Earth Shoes, drove small cars, and didn't use paper products. They believed mostly in triangles, like fidelity in a relationship was almost a negative value. Also you couldn't shave your legs. It was an anti-cigarette culture. You had to go canoeing. You had to know about the moon.

It was hard to capture because all that was implicit, felt Carol—the sense that this community did have these strong rules. Examples of the rules: there was a dress code. Levis had always been acceptable. No makeup. Hiking boots and track shoes, tee shirts and work shirts (or man's shirt kind of thing). Certainly the tee shirt was predominant. Overalls. That was your basic uniform. There were variations, like India blouses. But you had to make a conscious decision to do that, a conscious decision, for example, about what you were going to say when people said, "You're all dressed up tonight." But people did that, dressed up. People even wore dresses and skirts on occasion.

The community, felt Harriet, was made up of people who found solidarity and comfort in participating. She did think you had to consciously join it, but she didn't think there were any rules about being in it. It was basically an open association, except for the one requirement: that you had to be supportive of women who were trying to build healthy relationships with other women.

The community for her, said Jenny, was a place of belonging. At the same time she thought of it as very distant and hard-to-know. It was what she was supposedly part of, yet she didn't feel part of it.

3

Expectations of Intimacy

AN INDIVIDUAL VIEW

She kept trying to define the community, recalled Shelah, and not being able to, wondering if there really was one. She felt it was a group of people, a lot of times they were regulars, who agreed to identify with each other. As a working definition she thought of Natalie and Helen and their whole support group, a local lesbian version of "Our Gang." She supposed she had a love-hate relationship with it. It seemed to her to operate on a definition of a chosen few. It had a hierarchy, not necessarily a linear hierarchy, but a radial hierarchy: it was circles within circles.

She'd been involved with it for a little over a year and a half and for her what was crucial was that in this community, in order to know anybody pretty much at all, or to define yourself and become known, you had to give a considerable amount of what in other communities could be kept private. For example, people here were always defined in terms of each other, in terms of who they were lovers with or what kinds of relationships they had. That type of information was generally considered private. She resented that it had to be known. Yet a lot of times it was the way you had to go.

It seemed to her that women in this community, and women especially, got closer to each other by talking about each other. It was a way to get to know an absent person and a safe way of getting to know the person you were talking to. She did it, she talked about people, and then she found herself questioning herself as to what she should tell another person and whether it went by the rules she had traditionally thought of. "Which rules?" was the question. She thought there were somehow tacitly different rules in this community than there were in outer communities.

Talking about people in this community was not necessarily for the purpose of having power over them, as it might be elsewhere. Sometimes, though not necessarily, it implied a sexual interest. Talking about people was a way of getting your rocks off and a safe way too. Intimacy was maybe a better word for it. You talked about people you would not really consider having an affair with, but with whom it probably went through your mind to pass through that sort of thing.

It was really strange too, because when you spent a lot of time with a person and that person told you a lot and you talked about how you felt about yourself, and then you talked to another person, you wondered, "Should you share the information?" You considered, "What would it mean to tell?" You had developed a closeness with this first person and you wondered, "Would you be betraying this person?"

She didn't know how much of her concern about this came from her traditional upbringing. This community was constantly questioning traditional definitions of relationships, so maybe the rules she was raised with did not apply. A nuclear family in a traditional situation might go to a minister or a counselor or close friends or neighbors to talk about things considered private, for instance. Their whole community didn't have to know; whereas, in this community, talking about those kinds of things was a way for everyone to relate vicariously to everyone else. It was what was in common. In a way in this community you could get to know someone better by talking about them than by being with them because people here were really all so shy with each other. You needed a chaperone, a third person, to talk about things and take you through them.

This got back to the whole idea of what was a confidence around here. It was unclear. Unless somebody told her point blank, "Don't tell anyone," Shelah felt she just didn't know what to do with it. In many ways, she felt she didn't really care about what anyone knew about her, so maybe she took that as a clue that other people might not care either. In the sense that all this information defined the group as a community and you needed to share things and help one another, all the talk was not such a bad thing.

But there was a bad part about it and that had to do with the idea of violating, which had to do with being defined by your actions. You could resent being known only by what people were saying about you. Ironically, however, that forced a kind of privacy on you, in the sense that privacy was space to yourself that nobody either wanted to or could enter. This community could be a very lonely place if you couldn't see beyond that, Shelah thought. This was what had happened to her. She felt she had been defined very early by her comparative puritanism. People saw her as a cross between Mary Hartmann and Mary Pickford, and that had the effect of really limiting her in her relations with them.

She felt this because when she first came to this community, certain information about her previous relationship had gotten out. After that when people looked at her, she felt they were seeing somebody who didn't relate well to other people physically or erotically. Also, she hadn't fallen into bed with a lot of people in the community and that contributed to the definition. There was an expectation other people in the community had that she didn't: that had to do with this musical beds, the feeling that everyone slept around. Not being that way was something she felt real discounted for.

She also felt that there was generally a cruise-type atmosphere in this community and in the coffeehouses especially. It was not as bad as in the bar by any means, but in many ways it was worse because it was more subtle. There was a definite sexual tension. It was like good old sex being such an important part of people's lives and you came to a place with that expectation, like, "I am here because other people in this room are here because they have the same sexual orientation I do." This put great pressure on you as to what were you up to and what were these people in this room doing? There were all these sexual tensions and because of them nobody really got to know each other or to feeling comfortable with each other, or at least it took a while.

It had taken her literally months. She hadn't been involved with the community at first. It had taken her ten or eleven months after she moved here before she made herself halfway known. She hadn't come out into the community before that because she was embroiled in academia and she didn't even know there was a community. That was how accessible this community was. She found it through an advertisement for the campus gay organization in the university paper. Then she started coming to coffeehouses. Then she started feeling the cruise-type atmosphere and getting a sense of how people were defined in terms of each other.

For example, one of the first people she met was Millicent. Millicent took her to the bar, the old bar, Leo's. She told Millicent all about the relationship she had left in Maine. Millicent was shocked. She couldn't understand how someone could be so one-person oriented. Ever since that, she, Shelah, had felt defined in the community by her past relationship: that the relationship in Maine was "where we're coming from" and this gave an indication of "where we're going." She thought this because people in the community generally were identified by the kinds of relationships they had. This gave an indication of the kind of person they were.

She didn't know for sure that people in the community had made the definition of her she thought they had. No one said it directly, but she certainly got the idea. She got it from what other people would say at parties. She just felt this pressure to talk about her relationship with people she didn't know, to give herself an identity.

Not long after her talk with Millicent her relationship in Maine started breaking up and she talked with Hollis in the community. She felt that Hollis saw her in a very vulnerable place then, which made her uncomfortable still when she was around Hollis; she felt the same kind of powerlessness. She didn't think that was how she was all the time, but back then she had felt it strongly. She had felt she had no control. Her lover in Maine was leaving her. She felt rather incapable of handling her own action, no less letting someone else in on it. After she talked with Hollis, she had felt that the breakup and her past became fairly well known in the community fairly quickly.

Over time, it came to mean less and less to her that people knew, because it was later, because she had more control, but back then what she had felt basically was, "Help!" That was what she was saying to people then. And she felt totally alone. She was in this community, but totally left alone. All the bulwarks that supposedly worked for people here, they just weren't working for her. She thought maybe it was because she was different from most people in terms of backgrounds. Hers was that it was necessary to talk on a very pleasant level first before you got down to "I have had this relationship." It was just kind of backwards in this community: "I have had this relationship and, by the way, we both like macrame."

In this community you told people things to get identity in the only way it seemed appropriate at the time. You sort of sold yourself out in order to get a name or something. You needed the name, but Shelah wondered if you couldn't just start at another level. The way it was, you felt spiritually raped, especially in the context of this latent sexual interest. You felt, "Why were you telling this to someone? Did that mean you wanted to be intimate with them?"

There wasn't one woman in the community she hadn't considered having a relationship with, just because she was in this community and because of all the pressure to need and want a relationship. Because you were in the community and because you had to relate some intimate details to get along, there was always the question of whether you wanted to be intimate with the person you were talking to. In a straight community you had all these girl friends who you told things to, but in this community you had to worry about whether the sharing meant you wanted to go to bed with them.

A lot of the problem had to do with the latent sexual tension, which might or might not be there at all, but was expected to be there. Heterosexual society had taught everyone to look at prospects with people, and you came to this community and you did the same thing. It was the pressure of enforced intimacy. If you couldn't share bodies with people, at least you should be able to share information with them.

Over time she had gotten somewhat used to it however. It was different for her now than a year ago. It was different about her reputation for being a puritan, for instance. She hadn't had a whole lot of people approaching her. She hadn't let it get that far. A few people had approached her and she had said no. It was more that she was generally inhibited. Like at the party last Saturday night, Helen and Meg were going at her, teasing. They were kissing the hole in her shirt. They did it just to see how uncomfortable she could be. A year ago she would have been afraid of that, but now she liked the attention and she realized how trivial it was. She thought by now everybody had just decided this was not going to be foreplay or anything. Her responding didn't mean she was flirting. A year ago it would have meant it though, to her as well as to them. A year ago she might not have seen it as play so much, where now she kind of saw it as fun. A year ago she might have taken it more as the type of fun where a test would be included, where you wanted to test whether their idea of fun was the same as yours.

In general Shelah felt she had come into this community naive and lonely and she had sort of expected all that to be quenched. But that hadn't happened. In some ways her feelings of loneliness had gotten worse. She felt it was in some ways like high school here because of the sexual self-consciousness. She'd had a lot of uncertainty about how the system actually did work at first and she had felt more lonely because all her efforts to place herself in this community had to be a very singular effort, a very alone thing. You wanted to have an identity given to you and yet you had to do a lot of things to make that identity. At the same time, you had a lot of questions about how it was working, which made you really uncomfortable about the whole process that was involved.

By now, after a year and a half, she felt she had finally become known in the community as the "resident theater person." She was finally more in control of the label she got. She had worked for it. Part of her motivation to do performing this past fall was for identity in the community. She remembered doing her graduate recital at the university eight months ago. It was part of her program in theater. She put her recital together to make a personal statement in general, but she also wanted to expose herself: all this pain she had been feeling for herself and other people. One piece she performed (Judy Grahn's "A Woman Is Talking to Death") was a highly personal statement and yet a safe one. It was not a false thing. She was back there pulling strings, yet the strings were real. She wanted to say to that particular group of women, "I am here, you know." She didn't think it was a primary motivation in her performing, but it was there.

And this connected to one of the reasons she wanted to leave this community now. It had become a kind of mutual admiration society. There were too many laurels piling up for unknown reasons. She didn't feel there was enough stimulation or challenge. She needed another group. She wouldn't fault the community. She felt that her paranoia had dropped; their ignorance had dropped. But still she worried about the fantasies. Now she felt she had to be on stage more often, that they thought she must be good at parties. She felt more pressure to come through. It loosened the pressure to be intimate, but she didn't want to have to feel either: that she had to be up on stage or that she had to be intimate.

She was definitely more comfortable in the community now than she had been at first. It was a relief now to realize that she didn't have to have sexual feelings for other people, for instance, that she could have a friendship and she didn't necessarily have to fall into bed with them. There was also a kind of mutual respect that she felt had developed: for who she was, for who other people in the community were, for what their identities were. With that respect there came a more healthy type of relating.

4

The Web of Talk

There was this hotline that went around all the time, that kept the community together, felt Shelah. People were always talking about each other. It was not necessarily malicious, said Chip, but it was what traditionally was known as gossip. Things just went like widlfire, Leah observed. Gossip just spread really quickly, particularly with some people. There was a lot of gossip, said Emily. It was not ill intentioned. It was Hollywood-type gossip, infatuation—"Last night she was seen with her." She made hopeless attempts to control it sometimes.

Privacy? In this community? There was none, felt Jessica. You came into this community, said Martha, and at first you didn't want everyone to know your business. Then you found out that wasn't possible, or it wasn't the norm in this community. You found out that a lot of people knew your business, and that wasn't as frightening as you'd thought it would be.

The gossiping that went on, said Chip, she didn't like to put that on women: there was "discussion" going on. The gossip, the discussions that people gave, brought people in the community together and were supportive. They were more or less working with your feelings. They were trying to work it out. That was the kind of discussions she got into with friends. It was not character assassination which gossiping could be and which she felt went on more in other places where people didn't care so much about their community.

It was like a small town here, felt Alice. She came from a small town and she knew that there was a lot of talk in small towns. In both places, people had a tendency to think they knew a lot about other people. In both, they made a lot of assumptions, some of them correct and some of them not. But here it was different from a small town because people had more varied interests. In the community, it was not conservative nuclear-family types talking about football or how the Cubs did and being closed to new ideas and experiences.

She came from a small town too, said Ellen, and she had a sense that, like in a small town, a lot of people in this community knew a little about other people. They knew relationship kinds of things, employment kinds of things—like someone breaking up or wanting to change a job or something—but it was not in-depth. There was a lot less gossiping here than there was in the small town where she grew up. Where sharing information about other people as honestly as possible ended and gossiping began, she didn't know, but she felt that when she talked about people with other people in the community, it was usually with some kind of concern. Whereas in her small town her mother got together with her friends one or two times a week just to talk about people, and her father went to the bar and did the same thing. Women had coffee parties or bridge clubs or church clubs. She overheard their conversations. It was more a sharing of tidbits about people they knew but did not care so much about.

She loved that information got shared in the community, said Mitzi. She just loved it. She felt that she knew everything happening in everyone's personal life—not every fight and every detail, but all the big stuff, so that the larger moves in people's lives didn't come as a surprise. She thought everybody in the community knew something about the relationships other people had and how they were going: when there were bad times or just real good times. She felt that everyone learned a lot from hearing about other people, particularly about the hard times people had and how they worked them out.

That was important because a lot of times when a person would have problems or get angry it was set off by such a small thing, especially with someone with whom you had a primary relationship—like how she held a spoon. Often it was good to hear about other people getting angry at such tiny things because those turned out to be the real fights that ended up breaking up relationships. If you heard about other people, you didn't feel so much when you were having a hard time that you were wrong or right. You got a better idea that there could be miscommunication. It was always hard to accept that people were really different. You always thought, "We must all be thinking the same thing," and that was really not true, in this community especially.

If you went to a regular cocktail party with friends, thought Vivian, everybody was up—chat, chat, chat, chat, chat, chat. But if you went to a party in the community, they were just sitting around. They weren't putting up any sham or front. People here were more narrow in some respects than they were in other communities. Their talk tended to be narrowed to their own personal relationships, their own survival. She hadn't been to a lesbian party yet where people were talking about what was happening in the world or such. Now she was not saying they were not concerned, but the talk here tended to be more oriented to lesbianism and whatever that encompassed.

There was a period in her life, recalled Lilith, when she was just starting her relationship with Gayle. She was new to the community and she felt people were disapproving, that they felt she had taken Gayle away from Natalie. She felt she was told that at the time in nonverbal ways, like when she went to parties and people didn't initiate conversation with her; or if they did, it was just verbal chitchat, talking to her about weather and work, not the things that were "real" to this community.

She recently had her first lesbian relationship in the community, noted Bronwyn. Prior to this relationship, she was known as a straight woman in the community, and she hadn't felt she could say anything about her relationship with the man she was with. Then when she started relating to Meg, everyone wanted to hear everything. She had a new job at the time and she was really into it, but people didn't want to know about that. There would be a conversation and Meg's name would come up and she would see people's eyes light up. They were feeling "Tell us all these juicy things."

She didn't have a whole lot to say about her relationship with Meg because there weren't crises, which was a thing in this community. She felt it—the community—forced people into crises and traumas so they would have things to talk about. She also felt people in the community were relating to her real differently now than before because they knew she was willing to relate to a woman. This began to happen as soon as she and Meg started being seen together in public, as soon as they went to the bar. People began coming on to her. Also, they kept expecting her to have all these revelations about being a lesbian and she didn't have them.

She had been too isolated before, recalled Deborah, too private. She had been unwilling to share what she was, or who she was, with anyone. Then slowly during the past four months she had started giving more of what was going on with her. Before she hadn't talked to anyone in the community about herself, so no one knew good or bad of her, but now she was talking and, as a result, she was more vulnerable. People were able to touch her. She was just beginning to be able to speak. It was really hard. She could feel things, but they wouldn't come out of her mouth. It was like she had been silent all her life. The other night at a dinner at Sarah's, she had wanted to be more relaxed, so she stayed a little later; she stayed until she spoke to someone. Before, however, she had wanted to be alone, like Georgia O'Keefe, going off. She had stayed in her house alone for the past year.

During that year, she was in a relationship where she wouldn't talk to anyone about it and where she had felt extremely impinged upon to be asked. Then when that relationship broke up, she had found herself absolutely isolated and she went into the hospital. The hospital reminded her that there was such a thing as a community. After she got out, she got the next newsletter of the women's community and she knew she would go to anything they had. She went to a coffeehouse and if she heard of a group or an event, she would just begin to go to it. She would go to things and try to talk to people. At first, she was stumbling; she was mostly quiet. But then after a few months she began to let slip that everything wasn't really all right with her. Through that she began to meet a few people who were going through things, like their relationships were breaking up, and with these people she began to really speak about what was going on with her.

Since then she had come to value the community as a way of people maintaining contact with each other. She was still way out in the darkness, but she was slowly coming in. She had joined a support group three weeks ago (the one Lilith and Gayle formed) and she didn't speak there at first either, but just last night she spoke. She said she couldn't speak before, but she needed to speak now to change her patterns. Before she had thought that speaking would take away her power, but now she went home and she saw that it didn't. Before she had thought that when she spoke maybe the people in the group would have no response, but then afterward they hugged her. They also gave her support for different perspectives that might help her.

She had in her mind a movie, said Jessica. In this movie, everybody in the community was talking on the telephone to everyone else. She liked to think that it all meant something, that it wasn't just talking for the sake of it.

Her feeling, said Nikki, was that it was awful. She remembered running into someone in the community once on the city bus and they had this really superficial conversation that covered everyone in the community just about, specifically. When she got off the bus the whole thing seemed like a real violation. It seemed terribly small-town. It took portions of people's lives that were really meaningful to them and used them as diversions and entertainment, and that conversation wasn't malicious. She had heard of ones that were and those were real violations—like when someone in the community wasn't feeling good about someone else and they wanted to lend some credence to it by whipping out a certain fact and having the other person play around with that fact with them in the same emotional muck.

That bothered her a great deal. Another thing that bothered her was what would happen when you'd go to a party sometimes and people would be sitting around talking and they'd go through every name in the community. There was a smugness that accompanied that process. It was like everyone had been accounted for in the process of conversation. She didn't like it because it overlooked things that were probably the better part of who a person was. It made the individual the tool of security, of the security of the speaker and all of the people who were involved in the conversation. It was reductionist, reducing a person to less than they were; it was just not enough "for" the person.

That was, she thought, how the community trapped people into roles and behaviors in which they had no possibility to explore or to develop other parts of themselves that were different from the commonly known parts. That had happened to Earth. In the course of Earth's development in the community, she had gone through several phases that drew attention to her. People talked about them and Earth felt that fixed her in one particular stage of her development. If a new woman came into the community now, the same process would be in effect and she, Nikki, found herself wondering how that person was going to escape from the community. She herself had had the experience of feeling she was literally going mad when there were little pieces of talk going around in the community concerning her without her running along with them. What she did was to play little games to get around the violation. Whenever she sensed that there had been too many assumptions made about her, or if she felt there was an agreement made behind her back, whenever she ran into what that was, she would contradict it, flagrantly!

She had withdrawn from the community once, said Aurora, when it got to be too much. For three years she moved to a farm.

She would separate and talk to herself sometimes, said Jill. She might be in a noisy restaurant, she might be writing in her journal. Often the way her life was here, she didn't have the time or space to be alone, so she went inside. She would ask herself questions like "Well, Jill, how do you feel about that and what do you want to do about that?" It was during such times that she gave herself quality attention. She found that often her best thoughts came when there was a lot of noise outside and everybody around was talking or doing their own thing. Low-level noise outside made her concentrate more. It made her focus more on "Jill's thoughts." It was almost as if she was competing with them to get attention for herself.

At other times, though, she would physically go off. Last week she took this huge walk from the Women's Shelter all the way out to Lathrop Street. She actually did talk to herself. She asked herself questions. She told herself how funny she was and she laughed. She thought she would just go ahead and laugh with herself, even if nobody else might. It was so important, that type of situation—to be able not to care about being watched or seen.

She used to be very secretive in the community, recalled Diana. She was afraid of opening herself up But now what she did was to tell other people everything. She wanted them to know it all (this was people in the community, not at work). Like when things happened with her and Meg breaking up, she wanted people to know everything about it: from Meg's point of view, from her point of view. If they knew, then she wouldn't have to worry that they would make up stories and gossip and guess.

She had told people, said Natalie; she deprivatized her life.

In that way she felt she was different from most people in the community, because her world view had it that she gave up control. She didn't think she could control anything, particularly not information exchange among women. She couldn't control what people thought of her. She knew that a lot of people in the community didn't want information circulated about them because they would feel humiliated; they didn't want people to see this side of them. For herself, however, she thought most of the time she felt best when people knew all things about her, the weaknesses as well as the strengths, when they knew who she was. She felt that she had a basic trust that people were not going to hurt her. She also thought that people like her—who had been in the community longer—became aware that this was the entertainment here: that people talked about themselves and each other. They also became more careful about what they said. They reported hearsay as hearsay and made specific requests.

Marla, for example, had specifically asked people not to meddle. This, said Marla, meant she had asked them not to give information she had said about another person directly to that person, and not to give information another person had said about her directly to her. She felt that was destructive to relationships. In addition, there were certain things she preferred to keep private, to keep to herself. One of these was the fact that she was a witch, that she was psychic. She didn't share the specific experiences she had very much, even in the community: experiences like seeing spirits and hearing voices, being able to predict small events, having visions and hallucinations. Why didn't she tell? Because people wouldn't believe it or they would be fascinated by it. It was a funny combination of not wanting to be on display and not wanting to be interrogated, not wanting to be discounted or focussed on, either one.

Her spiritual beliefs and her whole view of the universe were not something she either frequently discussed with people or heard their views on. They were something she didn't want intrusions on. She simply didn't want to hear other people's opinions. She felt they were half-baked. She didn't want to deal with how they thought; it could be threatening to whatever kind of construct she had.

There were certain things that transpired between her lover Judith and herself, said Nell, that it was all right for certain people to know, but if suddenly a lot of people in the community were to know, she would be pissed at a lot of people who had been her confidants. There was this ring Judith had gotten for her, for instance. Judith gave it to her just the other day, with no strings attached. She, Nell, didn't want anyone to think that the ring represented anything else. She therefore thought it was best that people didn't even know that Judith gave it to her as a gift, because if they knew, then she would have to answer all the questions, like about the "no strings."

She had stopped talking about certain things in the community, said Ruby, because of how people would react. She had stopped talking about therapy and about having other friends. She did associate with straight people. She did go other places to have other perspectives, to get other parts of her nourished. She had a professional life. But this was not something she could talk about here, just as she couldn't talk about tennis. It so happened she had more skills at tennis than maybe all but two other people in the community, and they were fringy people, and that was a big part of her life. The same went for certain indulgences like drinking and smoking which none of her sisters would support, and for old forms of culture like opera and things that were considered elitist and bourgeois.

There was a time when she had shared more with people in the community, but in the last several years she felt she had come to share less, because as the community had grown larger, it had seemed to her harder to keep things in context. Let's say five or six years ago, if Natalie was divorcing her husband, there would be only four of five people Natalie would have to talk with about it. In addition, the people then weren't as aware of their choices; while now people had had time and a lot of exposure to different ways of looking at someone leaving their relationship. So now there would be some people who'd be very articulate about the value of long-term relationships, and some people who'd be very articulate about not spending one minute of your time with a man, and the people who expressed these opinions might in the process forget about Natalie and the pain she was experiencing. So their response would be out of context. Natalie would have disclosed something personal and people would be responding to it theoretically.

She had been in the community for about a year, recalled Madeleine, but she hadn't yet put a lot of energy into wanting to explore a sexual relationship with a woman in the community because of what she perceived as the "fishbowl." If she got involved with somebody, she wanted to be able to work it out without spilling her guts to everybody, and it was her perception that if you were seen with somebody else in this community, it was like in high school. If you were seen with that person twice, people thought you were intimate. How did she know this? From overhearing how other people talked about other people, and from asking questions sometimes. Because of not feeling in the core of the community, she had had to ask if some people were relating to each other or not, and some of the answers she got were more embellished than she felt she had asked for.

For herself, said Gloria, there was nothing she would hide. She didn't care if people in the community knew who she was relating to or when they made love. She did think, however, that it was important to be careful in terms of other people's privacy, like in a relationship she might have. She thought it was not appropriate for her to share information about her lover Leslie, unless Leslie felt that was okay, and it was important for her to establish what was private information about Leslie and what was not, or else she might share what she shouldn't. She and Leslie had said as a ground rule that unless you requested that certain information not be shared, it was fair game for her to share it. This had come up in the context of Leslie making love with someone else and her saying, "Could she share that?" and Leslie saying she could share it but not who it was with. It had also come up because Leslie didn't like information shared about the way she dealt with money. There were certain specific things Leslie was sensitive about that she didn't want to be teased about privately even when there were just two of them, or publicly.

The basic rule you learned from experience in this community, felt Emily, was that unless you stated specifically that you didn't want information passed, it got passed pretty quickly. That was something she had come to resign herself to. As long as it was not malicious, as long as it would not ostracize her, she could take it. But, there had been a period during the spring when everyone was changing relationships when it had seemed to her just too much. She had slept with Gloria during that time and the very next day two people called her at work. She had slept with Melissa the night before and Gloria the next night. The two people who called knew about them both and she, Emily, was stunned because she had told no one. She thought about it and figured, "Gloria talks a lot anyway." She assumed those people knew about Melissa because she had slept with her over at the house of Natalie and Jo who were central people in the community. Gloria knew about Melissa. The very next morning, Gloria confronted her with it when she saw her. Gloria, you see, used to be lovers with Melissa.

That whole incident was a great example of information spread, because pretty quickly it was common knowledge in the community: the fact that she had slept with Gloria was. Emily didn't know about Melissa. Fewer people knew about that. How did she know it was common knowledge? She was assuming. She assumed that everyone in Gloria's lover Leslie's support group knew about it because it was something Leslie had to work through. She assumed everybody at Lowell House knew because one of them, Bronwyn, worked at the Rape Crisis Center and was in Leslie's support group. It would go through Rape Crisis because a lot of information got passed there and also because the director, Valerie, was one of Leslie's best friends.

From the fact that Chip, who was one of the people who called her the next morning, knew, she, Emily, was sure that

Lucy (Chip's lover at the time) also knew—because you had to assume that any information that got passed would be shared with your primary partner if you were in a relationship. So generally she was assuming it was fairly common knowledge pretty quickly, within a day or so, though nobody ever said anything about it except those two who called. Nobody came up and confronted her and said, "Why are you sleeping with Gloria?" because it would have been rude. You didn't do that. You might gossip about people in this community, but you didn't directly confront them about something unless they had told you.

And these were just the people she was 99 percent sure of. The number, if you counted, was twenty-nine. Then if you figured the people that they were involved with, you had a cast of thousands. There were Mitzi, Jo, and Irene, who were good friends of Bronwyn who lived at Lowell House and worked at the Rape Crisis Center, and Deborah, who was a friend of Leslie's. That was four more. And then there were the people who lived in Gloria and Leslie's house, and the people on the volleyball team—that was eight or nine more—because Leslie, the second day after it happened, went and talked with Judith who was on the team, and Judith surely told Nell, her lover, who was also on the team. That was forty-eight people who she, Emily, could be pretty sure knew. She could be pretty sure in a week or two afterwards, though there were some people who were questionable, like Helen, even though she was in Gloria's support group; and sometimes people forgot because it was hard to remember who slept with who, because so many people slept with other people.

Plus Myrna knew because she was a friend of Gayle, who was head of the Women's Shelter and had a lot of ways to know, and Francis, who was in Leslie's group and was friends with Gloria, knew. If Francis knew, Vivian, who was her lover, knew. So it was fifty-one at least.

Amazing, wasn't it? Emily thought, for one harmless little

night. People were never judgmental. Nobody said "How could you do that to Leslie?" Except Leslie. Leslie couldn't handle it, so in the end she and Gloria stopped sleeping together. They made a commitment to Leslie the day after it happened that their relationship wouldn't be sexual anymore. That hadn't improved it, however. Leslie was still resentful and jealous of the time they spent together, and this was a couple of months later. And those fifty-one, those were only the people she knew knew.

Her own case, thought Jimi, was different. Not many people in the community knew that she was going into the air force soon. Maybe about seven to ten people knew. She had known about it since she had been here. Recently she was constantly surprised when she told someone and they did not know it. It seemed to her that it took a long time to become a stable part of this community.

Over time in the community, Natalie felt, you learned some things you didn't know at first. There was a question, for example, about how much people really did think would get out. People often assumed everything got passed on, that information got shared more broadly than it actually did get shared. They assumed all information was widespread, when the truth of it was that most people were pretty self-centered and talked about themselves and didn't spread a lot of other things. They only passed certain types of information and they talked mainly with those closest to them.

She was more with the bar group than the feminist community, Marie felt, but a lot of it was real similar, all the talk that went on, the gossiping. It was like how she felt after a one-night stand, how she felt the next day—as if she had been giving out secrets about herself. She thought people found out more about her, not necessarily during sex, but in the bedroom sitting and talking. It was like you had given yourself. You had said: "This is the total me. You have gotten to see me at some of my weakest moments, not necessarily my weakest but my openest." The intimacy was the main thing. You talked about a lot of things and you told a lot about yourself you just didn't want passed on or carried around. You didn't know how other people were going to take it. They might not talk about it the next day, but two or three years later they might say "I knew this woman. . . ."

5

A Sense of History

She had been around since the time the Women's Shelter first started, recalled Martha. The community, as she saw it, had evolved from one particular subgroup that was formed as a support group for the Shelter back then. That was about six years ago when Melissa and Elinor first started the Shelter as a refuge for women. A group of women from the larger community joined together in a support group to talk about the community functions of the Shelter. Over time that group changed gradually from a group that discussed straight women's problems and dealing with the men in people's lives, to a group dealing with a more lesbian set of problems, then to dropping the Women's Shelter connection entirely and splitting off to discuss more personal things.

Back when the Women's Shelter was first formed, recalled Lucy, was when she had first come out. At the time, she and a couple of other people sat down and listed all the lesbians in town they could possibly think of and there were sixteen names on their list. Martha remembered a time when she did the same thing and there were only eight. Both of them could still list all the names.

At about the time the Women's Shelter was starting, recalled Lucy, the Free Woman's House was also formed after three of them talked about it one night at the Shelter. That night was the first time she, Lucy, had ever been at the Women's

Shelter. She was a married lady and she thought, "Now these are lesbians and they don't even slick their hair back." She wanted to be in that house. She left her marriage and moved in a month later.

The community then, from what she knew, consisted of the people who lived in the Free Woman's House and the people who came to that house, except for Elinor and Melissa who lived at the Women's Shelter which was then located in Elinor's home. Natalie, who was now considered the leader of the community, was not yet out; neither was Gayle who Natalie first lived with. The others were speculating about them. A lot of women came out at that time by going to the Free Woman's House or the Women's Shelter, which existed as a refuge and a support group. The Free Woman's House ended a year later because there wasn't enough interest in having social functions at the House. There weren't that many people out at the time. (One-quarter of the community lived there.) The Women's Shelter continued, however, and the community expanded. It—the community—changed somewhere along the line from a student organization to a community-of-women organization—an organization of the women who were "out" in the larger community, who were faculty and everyone else. At the same time, the numbers of older women increased, older meaning older than twenty-two.

Activities evolved around the Women's Shelter at first, until the support group broke away from the Shelter about a year and a half after it started. Most of the activities were parties at individual homes or meeting at the Shelter, where Elinor was very concerned about having things be structured and there being rules and limitations. The support group at the Shelter varied in numbers, but just before it broke away it had about fifteen members.

The group broke away, said Marla, when some of the women who came to it regularly got tired of having new people drift in and out every week. They felt they needed to separate to build trust with each other. The group met after that at different individuals' homes.

After the group broke away, recalled Lucy, there were certain key people who entered, like Gloria who was a minister with one of the local churches. That brought in a kind of spiritualism and a concern with ritual which had also been developing from other sources. Gloria facilitated getting the meeting halls for the coffeehouses and the Womanspirit Celebrations. This helped to make the rituals more public and, after that, there were more community activities than something that might take place at somebody's house.

Gloria, who was a married woman then, remembered going to a party at Natalie's house where people were talking about wanting a lesbian space. She was wearing a long, fancy dress after having given an invocation at a state banquet. Melissa came up to her at that party and asked her if she was straight or gay. She said she was bi. She said she was from the church, that she understood they were wanting a space for women, and that she was there to offer them space in the church if they were interested in that. They took her up.

The support group, after it broke away from the Women's Shelter, said Lucy, met first on Friday night and then on Thursday night, which was when it began to be called the Thursday night group. The group wasn't closed then. It was open for anyone to talk about anything that was bugging them. It met at her and Chip's house as the Friday night group in the beginning and then burnt itself out due to negative conversations week after week. There was no celebration of good things, just how lousy everyone's life was. After that, it reassembled a little later when some of the people moved over into two Thursday night groups which kept going and which seemed to become a core of a certain kind of community. These two groups limited their memberships after a while so they could develop trust with each other and, over time, they became smaller, getting down to the long-term, stable kind of Thursday night group that existed now, with six or eight members in each. The newsletter came out of these groups and the Sapphic Plains Collective and the coffeehouses, in that these activities were organized by members of the groups.

One of the Thursday night groups that evolved from back then had more stability than the other, noted Martha, and seemed to become more central to what people thought of as the community. The two groups did connect however. What happened was both groups started having meetings at the same time at Natalie's house; one would meet upstairs and one downstairs. The joint meetings occurred every month or month and a half beginning a couple of years ago. That was when she, Martha, first started feeling there really was a community. She was in the "other" Thursday night group. After their formal meetings the members of both groups would all play together. Sometimes it was set up deliberately that they would meet together and play; sometimes it would happen by accident.

Out of that, something different arose. The summer before that fall when the groups started meeting together was the first time people had started fantasizing about the ideal community. Five or six of them did this. It started with stoned fantasies about taking over one of the parks outside of town. Mitzi had a fantasy that they'd all be living together in a huge house. They talked a lot about where people lived and about proximity and how important that was. They also started thinking about some sort of cooperative financial venture like starting a food coop. That never got anywhere however. Natalie was a real center. She seemed to have thought about what went into a community for a long time. She talked about it, let other people in on it. She essentially took over from Elinor, who had moved away a while before.

When the groups started meeting together, Martha recalled, there was a lot of talk about borrowing things from people in the community: a lawnmower, a list of tools people had they would be willing to let other people use. There was talk about some kind of community response to illness, to breaking up within the community. They wanted to find ways of not letting couples breaking up fractionalize the community because, for a long time, there had been sides and a lot of tension and having parties where one person couldn't come because the other was there. Then that summer that changed. People starting having parties and inviting everybody. Helen had a party at one point and the guest list included so many wars and feuds that she, Martha, remembered feeling she didn't want to go because it would be a circus. But then it turned out to be a nice party. That was in the summer two years ago when all these changes seemed to be concurrent, when the whole thing started flowing.

You could feel community more strongly in the fall, though a lot of it, Martha felt, had to do with personal needs. In her own case, she had been in a monogamous relationship which broke up during that summer and she was going through identity things about couples. Natalie and Jo were having an open relationship, so the support groups were talking about that sort of thing. She and Mitzi, her closest friend, were talking a lot about monogamy and nonmonogamy and she, Martha, just began to see herself as needing a group of people to meet the needs she had. Before, she had tended to get into monogamous relationships and distance herself from everybody else. Then her monogamous relationship would break up and she would be floating and would not know what to do with herself; so then it became obvious to her that she needed friends in addition to any relationship she would be in.

Then soon she noticed that her friendships came and went also. It seemed to her there was constant variation and nothing she could count on with individual people. So, given that she couldn't count on couple relationship or friendship, it seemed to her that if she was in a group, even if her relationships within that group were shifting, she could count on that group. Other people were talking about similar things at the time.

Another thing that affected it all, Martha felt, was "fair fighting," which gained in popularity during that time when the sense of community was growing. Fair fighting first came in a few years before (about five years ago) when Elinor and Melissa were having problems dealing with each other and with the Women's Shelter. They went to see Yetta in Michigan and came back with fair fighting skills. Yetta was one of the originators of fair fighting and a student of Bach's. She wrote a book called *Self-Care* which was big in the community, though it was not a good book really, Martha thought. (For specifying rules, *Aggression Lab* and *Intimate Enemy* were better.) When Elinor and Melissa came back, Elinor and Pearl, who was a therapist in town, started doing workshops and after that, at the Women's Shelter, there was a lot of talk of fair fighting.

The ideas of fair fighting appealed to some people in the community at the time because Elinor and Melissa, who were pillars of the community, were spreading them. They also appealed in terms of ethics. Let's say you had just broken up with someone and it had been a really rocky relationship in terms of games and you heard that you didn't have to play all those games—that you could be honest and ethical—those ideas would appeal. They also appealed to people like Earth for a different reason: because she was into rituals; she was a Catholic who hated Catholicism but still had good feelings about the rituals.

There was, however, a lot of resistance to fair fighting when it started, Martha recalled, because it was the period of Esalen and fads like primal screaming. Those hassles still went on, but the appeal of fair fighting was that it worked. As people picked up fair fighting skills, they managed situations that they hadn't been able to manage before. People picked up the skills by talking about it informally a lot, through the various waves of workshops that went on over the years, and through books that passed around. Elinor and Melissa were close with Natalie and Gayle, who were a couple at the time, so Natalie became one of the prime spreaders.

There was a workshop every six months for a couple of years and Natalie went to see Yetta a few times, but the workshops didn't matter that much. It was more people talking to each other. It spread through the support groups. Informal friendship groups started using it. There was a glossary in Yetta's book and the words started spreading. There were some adaptations, but not many. The words spread and once you picked up the words, you started doing the actions. Fair fighting seemed, after a while, to have a similar function in the community as the quotations of Chairman Mao in Communist China.

Fair fighting was a vocabulary and a way of thinking, felt Ruby. It was a way of dealing with yourself that was peculiar to this community, said Janet. If you went up to a bar woman in town and talked to her about fair fighting—if you talked about parameters of a relationship, or having your own space, or head space—she wouldn't understand. Once, for example, she, Janet, gave Mike, a bar woman friend of hers, advice on how to deal with her lover Lisa whom Mike was having trouble with at the time. Lisa had come out in the community. "Go up to Lisa," she told Mike, "and tell her that you 'need some space to deal with some issues' and she'll understand, rather than say 'Goddamnit, I'm going to get drunk' or 'I'm leaving.' "

Fair fighting, thought Helen, was a language, a style, that many of them in the community had been trained in. It was important, she felt, because it was an approach which valued relationships and valued people within them. It accepted the fact that people didn't always get along harmoniously and that there were some skills they could use to get along better and to take care of themselves. A good number of the women in the community, maybe thirty over the years since fair fighting was introduced, had been trained in it so they could be coaches in sessions when couples in the community had problems or when friends had problems. She herself was trained. Elinor and Melissa had introduced fair fighting into the community and probably if Elinor had wanted to teach Hindu, it would have caught on, Helen felt, but she would not have had the same opportunity. People started learning and seeing the utility in fair fighting, that it worked.

Fair fighting was important, Ruby thought, because it gave you permission to keep large chunks of yourself and your space intact and it ritualized negotiations to get privacy. In a fair fighting session you went through a "state of the union" message where you told where you were in terms of emotions in different areas. One of those areas was privacy, or separateness, in space and time. When you had a ritual to state your needs, you were more likely to get them met. A lot of this was in Yetta's book.

It was also in a paper that Helen wrote for a class at the university, said Sarah. That paper, titled "The Group," described how fair fighting was used in the community as a mechanism for conflict resolution which had as its basis the structuring of interaction between or among persons. Fair fighting was built, said Helen in her paper, upon three assumptions: (1) that a person was capable and responsible for taking care of herself; (2) that a person was responsible for representing herself and assumed others would represent themselves; and (3) that a person had and assumed control over her life, her actions, and only hers, not those of others. Fair fighting techniques were sometimes used directly between two people in the community, the paper noted. Sometimes they required coaches to structure interactions and make sure that the people heard one another and checked out meaning and to help them clarify their thinking. The employment of fair fighting as a ritual in the community, Helen's paper concluded, gave an indication of The Group's belief system: self-representation, self-care, control over one's life.

She thought, said Lucy, that fair fighting was not such a good thing in the community. It seemed to her that after a while it got so fair fighting vocabulary had to be used, in the support groups especially. Whether it was fair or not had nothing to do with it. Words that had to be used were: Vesuvius (for anger), commitment, time-limited, have an issue with someone, haircut (a little, bitty Vesuvius, like "Goddamn you really make me sick"), hook out, contract, bonding, primary, and responsibility.

She hadn't read any of the books and she didn't know if these words were official fair fighting words. They were what people in the community who did fair fighting said. It seemed to her that the vocabulary was manipulative. The norm was stability of relationships. It was used in the support groups when somebody disagreed: like when a peripheral person disagreed, they were always dismissed with a fair fighting technique such as "So-and-so was having a Vesuvius" or "That's not part of the agenda now." These techniques were mechanical ways of shutting up somebody. That was why she felt whether it was fair or not had nothing to do with it. It depended on who was fighting.

She thought, said Nikki, that fair fighting was the popular psychology in this community and that it was more distancing than anything else she had come across in relating to people. Theoretically, because of fair fighting, no one in this community had to worry about hurting anyone else's feelings. The person whose feelings were hurt had to worry about saying that their feelings were hurt. In her view, that was misplaced responsibility.

From what she had seen of it, said Harriet, fair fighting was important in the community because it encouraged non-romanticism. A lot of romantic notions involved taking care of the other person and losing control, like someone saying, "What do you mean? I had to do it. I loved her," as opposed to feeling that you were in control of your feelings and that you wouldn't do anything harmful to yourself or anything you didn't choose to do. Fair fighting was thus a way of taking the "I'm just a victim of love" kind of thing out of your life, because in fair fighting self-care was the rule. In this community, felt Harriet, you probably got more crap from being non-self-caring than for anything else. If you continued in a non-self-caring fashion for six or eight weeks, people lost patience with you or they lost interest. They assumed you wanted to suffer.

In her support group, said Lilith, they had recently been talking about trust and commitment being the primary positive feelings that were important to have for another person, rather than romantic love.

Such things were relatively new, however, felt Ellen. Many of the activities that people in the community now took for granted, like the newsletter and the coffeehouses, were also relatively new. They started only a couple of years ago. In the beginning there wasn't even a gay bar in town.

There was one straight bar that people went to then, re-called Diana, a bar which now had a different name. Then there was this other bar they started migrating to, which was also straight and which also had since changed its name. Then the first gay bar—the Carousel—opened five years ago and there was an upsurge in social life that centered around people who hung out there. Then the Carousel closed and Leo's opened, but Leo's was never the women's bar like the Carousel had been. It was small and dingy. When the Orbit opened just this past year, people started going over there. The Orbit was larger, a more disco-type of bar, and better than Leo's, but still not like the Carousel.

When the Carousel closed two years ago, remembered Judith, all of a sudden the women had no bar they could call their own. After that, every Friday night for at least two months there was a party at somebody's house. More than their share was at Alice and Lucy's. That was, in a way, how the parties got started as a focus of the community.

Then came the groups, all the groups there were now, recalled Ellen. There was the Sapphic Plains Collective, which organized certain things including the newsletter and the coffee-houses, and the choir, which began when Helen was talking in her support group one night about wanting a choir but not doing anything about it. Marla was mad at Helen for Helen's thinking she might get back together with Meg, who she had just broken up with, and so Marla gave Helen what in fair fighting was known as a haircut. Helen's haircut was to form a choir. There were also the support groups, three of them now; the sports teams, two of which were primarily lesbian; the Memorial Day picnics and the rituals—the May Day, the Seder, Thanksgiving, and the Womanspirit Celebrations.

A lot of the impetus for the rituals, recalled Martha, came when Marla became interested in rituals and, along with Earth and Gloria, felt they had something to do with creating solidarity and defining the group. Then each year the rituals would change.

As for the coffeehouses, they also were different now than they had been at first. At first there would be a total of ten people who would come to the coffeehouses and they would stay for only an hour or so. When you came, there would be maybe five people there. The coffeehouses were discontinued at one point. Then they started up again and for some reason the attendance was way up, maybe because they started having booze at them. This year they were up to thirty people each time, with a few big meetings to talk about community issues when forty to fifty women came.

Things that used to be closed in the community were now open, noted Lucy, like the May Day celebration and parties. Parties themselves went through a big transition over the years, recalled Martha: from closed (invitation list); to called "open," but what this meant was you had to be discrete when you invited anybody (which for a while meant it was understood that there were some people you wouldn't want at your party, that you wouldn't just go to the bar and announce to everyone that there was a party); to called "open" with less strings; and finally to being announced in the newsletter.

When people were in the community longer, they knew some of these things, said Natalie; they had seen the community operate more. Yet there was this assumption that people made, especially people new to the community, that the community had attitudes, that the community thought certain things. Strictly speaking, however, there wasn't a community here yet, in the sense of there being a really committed group, except for maybe a half dozen "true believers"—people who when you talked to them showed the same sense of knowing what it was. True believers were those who believed that they wanted a committed survival group to continue over time and to grow and who knew that they had to work to make that happen and that they had to commit things to one another. In this group, Natalie would include herself, Marla, Mitzi, and Jo. Jo was not conscious yet, but she was living it. There were maybe more than six. There were Lilith and Gayle. Gayle seemed to have it, but you couldn't trust if she would stick with it. Earth had been one before she left. And of course there was Ellen.

There was also others like Martha, Gloria, and Helen who had a lot of the concepts but hadn't committed to it yet, and there were others like Lucy who came in and out. It was rather like a religious community, and the women who had been there the longest were the church elders. The longer you were in it, the more you were invested, the more careful you got about the community as your home base and the more you cared about its being in harmony. You got used to the fact that information flowed, that the subgroups affected it, that there were certain rules, like fair fighting rules.

People just starting to participate, thought Martha, would find that the structures were there already on some level. Their sense of the community might keep them from resenting some lack of privacy within it.

There was a conscious concept of community they might come to have, felt Natalie, as different from in an unconscious way being part of a support system. Newcomers, a lot of new women who were just looking for lesbian friends, they didn't have that consciousness of community yet.

PART II

6

Parties and Gatherings

Parties were a time to catch up on what people were doing and to feel part of the broader community, felt Helen. She enjoyed getting ready for them, spending time on planning what she was going to wear, and fixing up. She didn't get really flashy, but she wanted to take care. She enjoyed parties because they gave her a chance to mingle with people in the community whom she might not see otherwise. She liked to play at parties, to have a good time. She liked being recognized by people and recognizing them. By "recognize," she meant given a nice greeting, for example, a hug or a very warm "Hello" or "How are you?"

Parties, felt Lucy, were the single strongest breakdown of barriers between people in the community who might at other times just gather in cliques. At parties you went around and talked to people you didn't get a chance to talk to anyplace else.

They were a time for being out in public, said Mitzi. Usually when she went to a party she liked to be alone, to do what she wanted and spend time as she wanted with people, also to leave when she wanted to leave. She saw parties as times when spontaneous things happened and she liked to be able to go with those things. She liked to know she could have those times and not have to ask permission of a person she'd come with or be considerate of them.

She liked to feel she could act natural at parties, said Ellen, or at the bar. She liked to just float. She liked to be in the woodwork and to come out of the woodwork. She didn't like to be pinned down as so-and-so's lover, even when she was. There was something about relationships, that she felt vulnerable about them around other people, that she felt uncertain. She liked to be flexible in the minds of outsiders. She liked to be by herself. She didn't like to have to be responsible for anyone else. It worked out well now going places with Marla. They each already knew a lot of people in the community, so when they went to something, they would each go their own way. It was like they came came together, but they were alone.

Her involvement with the community when she first came here, recalled Sarah, was mainly through Helen who would take her to parties. At the time she, Sarah, was having difficulty allowing any merging of herself with any other person or group. She thought she wanted the merging in a deep emotional way, but she felt that her freedom to be whoever she might most happily be required that she reject Helen and that she keep a distance from the emotional heart of this community. So all through her first months here, while she did go to parties and was casually socially part of things, she held back. She would not let people penetrate her casual sociability. She maintained a private space that was very lonely, often unhappy, yet nonetheless proud in its own existence. She had a split life of private misery and public sociability, but what was important was that she learned she could get along. There were little skills she never had to use so much anywhere else before that she found herself using here, like just being nice to people and agreeing with them in a surface way. She had to exercise those skills in this community because she felt her whole life depended on it. It depended on her being polite in a profound sense.

When she went to events at first, said Jenny, mostly parties and coffeehouses, she had this feeling that she was infringing. She almost stopped going because of that. She'd go to the coffeehouses and everybody would be sitting around talking and she would feel out of place. It seemed to her that the group was closed and that they were a little afraid. She had felt the same way at other times herself. She had seen someone new and then felt threatened. She came from a small town not far from here, and one of the reasons she had moved here was that everybody there knew her business. As a result, she had felt invaded. Now she didn't want to move back there, but it had been kind of hellish for a while: she felt funny back there, she felt funny here. Then she started playing vollyball. It was easier for her to become friendly that way—when she was active in something where she could participate and become competitive—while at parties or social-type events, she felt she had to be totally reserved.

She really wanted to be more open. She had been thinking for a while of getting more involved, but she had a fear, a protective device. What was she afraid of? That people would find out about her private self: her, Jenny. That what they found out could be used against her. It was hard. The whole thing was really hard. She wanted to be open and honest, but at the same time she was afraid.

When she went to her first party in the community, recalled Carol, it had started with the fact that she had been taking a class with Helen at the university in the fall. Originally she had been invited to this party by Helen. Then she was disinvited by Helen because Helen wasn't sure she was a lesbian. She was reinvited after that by Sarah who was also new in town. At first she didn't know if it was the same party, but in retrospect she felt she should have figured out that in this community there would be only one party on a Saturday night. She went to the party with Sarah. Helen was there and seemed somewhat awkward. Later she felt that whole series of events gave her a clue to the fact that this was an exclusive community, and that bothered her because she felt that her credentials were being questioned and that you had to have credentials to be part of this community. Also, at that party, she had been disappointed because she couldn't identify with the women there as she had with the women back where she'd come from in California. She didn't feel as wide a range of acceptance. She decided she wouldn't cultivate being a member very much after that.

In the winter, however, she got involved with a woman who was more active in the community. This was Shelah. The two of them would get invited to things. There was one party they went to at that time, a Christmas party, which was also an awkward situation because another woman, Toni, whom she, Carol, had an involvement with was there as well. She and Toni were just friends because Toni was married and had a very complicated personal situation, but Toni was pretty demonstrative.

There was this one scene at the party that began with Toni talking about wanting to dance and ended with Toni and herself getting into this close, slow dance with a lot of body contact and intimacy, and Shelah was directly in the background, and behind her was Bronwyn, Shelah's housemate. It was then that she, Carol, realized that this would be misinterpreted public exposure. She had assumed there was public display at parties in the community, but she didn't think there was usually as much as this. She also had a feeling of being unfaithful to Shelah, even though she wasn't really doing anything.

This suggested something she felt about parties in general in the community: that they were very formalized behind all that laid-back, casual atmosphere, though she was not sure she had been at enough of them to judge. She had been to holiday things. People got dressed up, but it wasn't that. It was about the contact. People were well behaved, very well behaved at these parties. In another kind of context the way she had danced with Toni might not have been noticed. It hadn't bothered her at first, until suddenly she realized that this was the wrong place to be doing that. It was like being naked on a bus, which raised a whole lot of things for her as to why she felt this community was so highly regulative and restrictive.

The whole structure of the community was behind the parties and the coffeehouses, felt Millicent. The structure operated a lot of good things that did a lot for people, but the structure didn't deal too well with individuals. The community didn't deal too well on an individual basis. She had in mind the first party she had been to in the community three years ago. There were maybe thirty people there. It was a brunch at Natalie's house. She had never been to a lesbian party before. She was introduced to a lot of people there, but they didn't say much to her, so she had a negative feeling and a feeling of being inferior to them. That was not anything they gave her verbally, because certainly they did not say much to her. It was more a result of her feeling, "Why aren't they saying anything to me?" She thought she must not be as good.

Then later she got active in the gay organization at the university. She organized the Gay Speakers Group and the Gay Phoneline and was politically active and people started talking to her more, but still she remembered that first time. She knew a lot of women she introduced into the gay life style who, if they had gone to just one party or a coffeehouse like some of them were, would never have come back, because they would have seen it as a closed group.

When she first became involved, recalled Francis, she was married. Her husband was an army officer and they had three kids, three boys. She had identified as a lesbian since she was in eighth grade, but she had always been in the closet. She had been seeing a therapist and one day that summer she screamed to her therapist that if she didn't get out of the closet, she would suffocate. Her therapist, Pearl, was familiar with the community and arranged for her to have breakfast with Natalie, whom Pearl knew from the old days of the Women's Shelter. Pearl knew that Natalie had been married and had chosen to leave the marriage for a lesbian life style. She, Francis, then met with Natalie and Natalie suggested she talk with three people: Ellen who was out of town, Myrna who was in town and married, and Earth, because Natalie had the impression that Earth enjoyed helping people out of closets. It was actually Earth who told her about the coffeehouses.

She went to her first one one Friday night and she was totally freaked out. The last time she had come out of the closet was when she was in college and a friend of hers introduced her to the bars. Back then it was the butch-femme scene and she had refused to get involved because of that. When she went to this coffeehouse, she saw everyone in coveralls. She had on a blue polyester suit and she felt like a sore thumb for one thing. Then Natalie started showing pictures she had brought from somebody's prom in which there were two lesbians: one wearing a tux and one wearing a formal gown. When she, Francis, saw that, she thought, "Yuck! There's no difference from 1962." She literally got nauseated and had to leave. She asked Natalie to sit with her out on the couch in the lobby until she could calm down.

After that, two of the women, Gayle and Lilith, invited her to a party out at their house and that was different, a whole lot better. In the meantime she had contacted Janet and they were talking. Then, with the encouragement of Lilith and Gayle, she went to the big summer music festival in Michigan. She was scared to death. For the first time she was going into this situation with no holds barred: just being with women for four days, driving with a group from the community. Then the festival itself was instructive from an introspective point of view. It made her realize that she was not a separatist, that she didn't automatically identify with groups but with specific individuals, that she didn't identify with all lesbians necessarily.

In her case, she first came to the community two years ago, said Stephanie, when she was still in high school. She came through Marla, who she had known from before either of them came out. For the first year she was getting to know people and trying to fit in and drinking. That was her last year in high school. Then she started going to coffeehouses and parties. She would go and stay for short amounts of time. The time got longer as there got to be more people for her to say hello to and talk to. It was hard though, because there were maybe twenty women she identified with, but she didn't really know them. Just getting to know people took time. Just being able to be articulate and keep a conversation going when she didn't know a person or have anything in common was the main thing she had to learn.

She felt, said Jill, that it happened slowly. For her it was still happening. She felt like a novice, a newcomer. Maybe it was just a matter of finding where she fit in. To her, at first, it had felt like the community was surrounded by a membrane that was impermeable. After a while she thought it went two ways: you had to do something to enter; it wasn't all up to them. But still she would feel a problem because you couldn't just go up to people you might see at a party or an event and ask them, "What's the story of your life?" Yet that was her first question. She didn't need the whole story of their life, but she wanted something that told her about the person in a significant way, like, "I always wanted to own a Mercedes."

She just hated the parties in the community, said Leslie, especially the big ones. She ended up being stoned. She liked just watching. For her, it was easier to deal with people one to one. It was more concentrated, more central, not as confused as in a group where it became superficial. At parties you had a few fleeting discussions with people and you hugged a few waists and it was just like at the bar, though she had found if she did get into more of an intense conversation with someone off to the side, she would feel more okay. She had been known to leave parties, to slip out, to get tired of them and just leave. There were little interactions everywhere at parties and she just didn't like that. She got uncomfortable with it. She would leave early and avoid all the hugging. Sometimes she felt that people would hug her simply because she was with Gloria, so sometimes she would make it real clear that she just wanted to shake hands.

She was thinking, said Nell, of the party last Saturday where she and Judith were really drunk and stoned and hanging on to each other with their arms around each other and her son Dudley was around. After that party she got to thinking of how, in the beginning in the community, she had been concerned that there were certain people who didn't trust her because she was married. Now there might be certain people who would think, "Are these people who are carrying on like this in this party with this kid, aren't they modeling themselves after this old heterosexual pattern?" because it was heterosexuals who tended to hold hands going down the street. They tended to enjoy exhibiting their affection. At their parties there was more coupled behavior. People in this community, however, had a desire to distinguish themselves from heterosexual behavior. There was this ideal that Natalie had of more community and less pairing: the idea that people who entered into a more or less monogamous situation were simply patterning themselves after what people ordinarily expected the principals of a heterosexual family to be doing, and that it should be different here.

She thought, said Mitzi, that a lot of people in the community had had something like this happen in their experience with parties: they became primary with someone and then they went to their first party together and they stayed on opposite sides of the room. For the first five hours they didn't talk with each other, they didn't dance with each other. It was like they wanted to prove they were balanced, were independent, could be okay socially without the other person, didn't have to be a clinger. It got complicated, in addition, when women related to more than one woman and they were all at a party together.

When this had happened to her, she had dealt with it by talking with the person she was going to the party with beforehand. They would talk about their expectations of party behavior. Then what she liked to do when she got there was to pretend that they hadn't come together. That was often hard, however. With Natalie recently, for instance, it was hard to go to a party and stay apart and not hug Natalie and not kiss her. The whole community knew. It had been a year since they had been relating, but they hadn't had one kiss in public. It was like they were walking on nails. They were not wanting to be really intimate and be necking in public, so they went to the other extreme and never even kissed.

About a month ago they finally decided that it would be okay to hug. When it came to doing it though, they would wait until everyone left, and there was a shyness about it. Nonetheless, it was something. It had taken a long time to get this far. She and Natalie had started trying to work it out six months ago after one party when they first started to talk, just admitting they felt a problem, like, "This is it." That happened because in that party and the one before she had found she was getting no eye contact from Natalie, so she started giving Natalie no eye contact. There were other examples, too, like they were having no conversation with each other at parties, they weren't touching. It all began to be very obvious at that point, so they started talking about it.

Then there was another party. At that one they had eye contact and a lot of smiling and waving "I'm okay" from across the room, but it wasn't okay really, because in reality if they had been acting normally, the way they acted with friends and each other in other places, there would have been more conversation, anything. All they had now was smiling and waving to each other from across the room. They were still staying away from each other.

Then at the next party, at Helen's on New Year's Eve, they worked out some specific things beforehand that they were going to do. One was that one of them would initiate talking to the other one for fifteen minutes. That first person would come up and ask, "Is this a good time for us to talk?" Then later the other person was supposed to ask for a dance. Through the evening you each had to do one thing. They thought they could rearrange it at each party.

That strategy seemed to help. It helped that they had to dance together. It helped having the conversation. After they tried it that way a few times, however, they realized it was really hard at parties to set up asking for those kinds of behaviors without being spontaneous. It was hard in terms of the conversation, because if they set up talking for fifteen minutes and some- one else came up to them wanting to talk, they would feel that was not all right, because they really had wanted it to be a little alone time between just the two of them. The dancing part was hard too, because as it worked out, they would end up spending a lot of time and energy focusing on whether the other one was dancing. She, Mitzi, would keep looking at whether Natalie was dancing and Natalie would keep looking at her, and dancing really didn't start until the end of a party. They soon began to feel that probably it would have been better just to sit in each other's laps then to go through all that, so they decided to talk about it again. By this time they had been paying attention to hearing about what happened with other people who might be having a similar problem. They had also been watching other people and seeing what they did. Finally, at that last talk, they decided just to act like they would normally, or the way they acted at parties with everyone else except each other.

As a result, after six months, the initial problem had gotten a little better. Whatever happened, they had a process to work things out. The way they behaved at parties was more natural now. She, Mitzi, had felt this at the Seder at Marla's last week. At the Seder several times she and Natalie would pass each other and touch and say "Hi, you're my friend." They were touching everyone else. It felt really good, like breaking the ice, "Oh, we touch." There wasn't any tenseness through that whole evening. They didn't have to spend a lot of tension always checking in on the other person to see where they were.

She used to have a harder time, said Ellen. Before, when she was lovers with Andy, Andy had a real successful party behavior, and when Andy would get going it would be hard for her. She, Ellen, would feel some competition, like when Andy would make jokes or butt into a conversation and say something smarter than she would. Andy didn't see it as competing, but she did, so she'd fall asleep. She got a little reputation for that.

When she first came here five years ago, said Gerry, she was invited to a few parties and she felt they were boring, so she told her lover Cynthia she wanted to have a party that was different. She made a list of who would come and it got to seventy. She couldn't fit that many people in their trailer, so she decided to have a picnic. She wanted to avoid the situation where when you had a party and you wanted to invite somebody, the first reaction of people was "Is so-and-so going to be there?" She started planning a picnic out in the woods so that if there was someone people didn't want to see, they could have acres and acres of land. She went around and started preaching, trying to get people to come, and that was the start of the Memorial Day picnics.

Lots of people came to that first one and when it was over, she was struck with two ironies of it. One was that after they had found this place in the middle of nowhere (because people were worried about being gay), the place was so secluded they couldn't find it again the next year. The second was that people everyone thought didn't want to be in the same room spent all their time together. People who hadn't talked to one another for six months to a year were sitting there talking to each other. It was great!

There were some events in which she felt more relaxed than others, said Aurora. She felt better at the Memorial Day Picnic and helping Ruby move. There was something about eating with other people and playing with them and helping them move that you sort of blended easily.

There was a time, recalled Leah, when she was saying good-bye to Jimi within a week of when she started saying hello to Ginger. Jimi was mad at her because Jimi thought Ginger wasn't letting her say a full good-bye. At that time it was really awkward for her to be with Ginger near Jimi in public. She and Ginger couldn't act like they wanted to because they felt that Jimi had told some of the women in the community about what had happened and that these people had a negative idea based on that. It was the beginning of her and Ginger's relationship and they felt it was real beautiful, real pure. They didn't want people badmouthing it, so both she and Ginger, to protect themselves, wouldn't be real physical, would be real reserved, would contain themselves at parties. This was also because they didn't want Jimi creating a scene and stalking out.

In the beginning, thought Ginger, it must have looked like she got involved with Leah and stole her away from Jimi. At parties people would say "Who's Leah?" (Leah had been pretty removed from the community before.) The follow-up comment would be "I thought she was with Jimi."

Her breakup with Leah, Jimi felt, went through the community much more quickly than their getting together. She thought it might have had something to do with the public nature of it. At the time of the breakup they had some uncomfortable discussions in large groups—like at the Christmas party at Judith's house, they had some very uncomfortable discussions inside and some yelling on her part outside, some pounding on the car. When they were first together, however, neither one of them was really part of the community. She hadn't been part of it because of the slowness she had felt, the sense that people here didn't trust. It took a long time for them to feel safe in extending themselves to include you.

She, too, had felt turned away at first, recalled Opal, but then she became involved with Bart, who lived in another town and knew some of the women and was older. She met Bart by going to a party once and immediately felt a kinship with her. She also felt scared at that party. She was generally scared socially, so she probably wasn't doing all she could have, but nobody reached out to her except Bart. She guessed she was scared because she felt that a contact at a party was a sexual thing. If a person were to call her up afterward, they would really be saying "Hi, you wanna fuck?" Her fear was that if someone approached her, that was what they would be meaning. It was generally unfortunate too, because what she really would have liked to do was to be able to relate to another woman sexually as

an initial building-block thing, not as something that was reserved. But that seemed virtually impossible. What she was
scared of, then, was the whole thing that made it all not up-front.

In the hospital community where she was before, said
Deborah, it was much less judgmental than here. If you wanted
to walk around and call yourself the Lone Ranger and wear a
mask like one guy did, nobody would hassle you. No one would
ask, "Why are you acting this way?" They would say, "Hey,
Lone Ranger, come play pool or have a Coke or something."
While here, though they accepted a wide range of things, you felt
that they made judgments, like about what kinds of relationships people should have: whether they should be monogamous or nonmonogamous, whether you should have men in
your life, whether you should stick together or not. These judgments were there when people got together, even if they weren't
talked about. Ideally the lesbian community aimed for being
nonjudgmental, but people still had these strong feelings.

Another thing that was different was that in the hospital
when you went in, you threw away your independence. They
locked the doors on you. You had to take the pills they gave you.
You followed the rules. The worst thing had happened: they had
locked you up. You were all in there together. Nobody was better
than anybody. You had all failed in the outside world. You
could relax with that. Then you could get beyond it. Whereas in
the lesbian community, you had to make it seem like you had it
together, especially at larger social events. There was not that
universal admitting of how frail everyone was, how in need,
how not together. In the support groups and where you met with
friends individually, there might be more of that admitting, but
not at parties or when you went to the bar. You were cool, you
know.

The community, for her, had been a lot to take at first,
recalled Jill. She didn't have anything in her background like it.
Here all of a sudden she was thrust into this supportive atmosphere. It was like they were saying "Well, here it is, open up,

kid." It took a while for her to feel she could open up if she wanted to and be quiet if she wanted to. She felt that in this community there was a lot of human caring. There was a lot of feeling that members of the group had for one another. It took a while to feel that it really was caring, but in the end, because it was genuine, the support could be felt.

7

Couples

Since she had been alone, said Kelly, she had felt a lot better, because she had a tendency to do things when she was by herself. When someone else was around, she had difficulty detaching herself.

When she first met Hollis, recalled Sam, she had told Hollis about her relationship with Mary Jean: how, in effect, she was just hanging around until the right man came along for Mary Jean. Hollis listened and did not approve, she felt. Hollis accused her of not being a separate enough individual in that relationship.

She and Deidre had gotten lost in each other in their relationship, felt Claire. That didn't become noticeable to her at first until she started having other personal needs and certain rumblings hit her in the face. Then it struck her that her "I" had gotten lost in the "we" of Diedre and Claire and that neither of them knew which of the needs they had were real ones and which were needs based on fear. What she was feeling now was that each of them needed to have their own place, so they wouldn't get lost in the structure of the living-together situation.

She'd had boundary problems with Meg, felt Helen. She hadn't had good walls up. She had allowed Meg to come in and it took its toll on her. For example, if Meg were sad or upset, she would drop anything, literally anything and go off and be with her. What she thought she was doing was showing Meg that she was a constant and what a good person she was, that when Meg needed help she would be there for her. But what she had actually done was to not let Meg learn to take care of herself, and to not take care of her own self.

There was a pattern to her relationship with Meg, Helen felt, that was similar to the pattern in her relationships with other people. She had trouble saying no. People were in there, in her space, too much and too often. She wasn't having room for herself. The pattern was not having boundaries soon enough, early enough, in relationships, and then having to put them in later.

For her it was different, felt Meg. She didn't have difficulty saying no to people who wanted to spend time with her. She made immediate judgments. She had very few friends. As a writer (and she said "writer" but actually she meant "poet"), saying no was the only thing she could do and remain alive. She absolutely had to have the time. It was part of why Diana said they were breaking up. Diana, who she was lovers with now, felt that she, Meg, was not social enough. But Diana had no sense of privacy. Diana felt that when they were out together it was private time, while she, Meg, felt only when they were home together and shut the door and turned off the phone was it private time.

An example of this was when she and Diana would have private time set up for an evening and somebody would drop in and Diana would say, "Why don't you stay for dinner? There is plenty of food," and she, Meg, would get upset. Or they would start out to have private time, just being together in an evening, and Diana would say she had to go to a meeting. They'd be sitting there and someone would call and say, "We're having a meeting," and Diana would say, "Oh, I forgot," and get up and go. She would say she would be back in an hour, but the time would have been broken.

Meg would ask for time, "quality time" was what she called it, said Diana. She, Diana, thought that meant their being able to sit and talk, but they usually ended up fighting and that was a hell of a way to spend a Saturday night: to sit there crying. For a while they had it set up so that each weekend one of them got Friday night and the other got Saturday night to plan what the two of them would do together. Then the next weekend the nights would be switched. But somehow it always happened that on Meg's night there would be a coffeehouse or a party. Meg wouldn't say no, but she'd get angry, and Diana would then feel that she was getting punished.

It could have worked, but it didn't, Diana thought. Maybe there was something about her own not wanting to be alone with Meg. Maybe she was avoiding trouble, because so many times when she and Meg would be alone together they'd fight and she thought if they had other people around they wouldn't fight. Or when they were alone together they'd go off into their rooms and be separate so they wouldn't really be together. That was Meg's complaint. Another part of it, she felt, was that it was hard for her, Diana, to relate to another person one to one where you sat and talked and you didn't talk about the weather, so she tended to avoid it.

Also, she would feel that they were together all the time, that they had plenty of time to talk. In a way, she just never really knew what Meg meant. It was as if Meg was always wanting something she wasn't getting. If it had been only Meg's need for privacy and her own need for people, it would have been all right, Diana felt; she could have done her socializing outside the relationship. But it seemed threatening to Meg when she had friends or did anything outside other than work. Because of this, she, Diana, felt closed in; she felt not trusted by Meg. It was as if Meg couldn't take her love for granted, as if everything was a sign that she didn't love her.

So in the second year of their relationship, she did what she felt was a terrible thing. She started socializing outside the relationship and the terrible thing was she started tiptoeing around and hiding what she was doing, trying to accommodate Meg and, at the same time, hating Meg and hating herself and being unhappy. When she finally would do something outright and tell Meg, Meg would be hurt and get angry and she, Diana, would be feeling, "Look at what I have done for you. It was just this one time." Then she would get angry back at Meg and start hating Meg and doing things that made Meg feel miserable and crazy and ugly and just an unpleasant person.

At times like that she would tell Meg she felt Meg was crazy. She wouldn't be able to let Meg know she understood her pain or to comfort her because she was so angry, because she had been denying herself. What had happened since then was that she'd had to learn to say "I must" and "I want" and to do what was important to her. She'd had to realize that just because someone else was uncomfortable with what she wanted to do was no reason for her not to do it.

It was true, said Meg. She was easily threatened in her relationship with Diana. She felt a lot of jealousy. She didn't want to feel it. It wasn't a desirable quality about herself. It was like a weakness, something she didn't have control over. When Diana told other people about problems in their relationship, she felt that was okay because all people had problems. Most of them wouldn't make her seem crazy, except the jealousy thing. She never could tell if she was just being paranoid, or if Diana was actually doing the things she feared. It would get messy sometimes. Let's say Diana would want to have lunch with someone who was an old lover but not old enough and Diana would ask if that would bother her. She, Meg, would tell Diana yes and Diana would say, "Oh, I won't have lunch," and then ask her a lot of questions about it, when really she should have had lunch.

About a year and a half ago, recalled Diana, she and Meg started seeing a therapist when it got so there weren't any areas in which they felt comfortable anymore. They saw Kathryn, a therapist for a number of women in the community.

She saw Diana and Meg, she saw Natalie and Jo, Lilith and Gayle, Elinor and Melissa. She saw the whole community at times, said Kathryn. From what she saw, the problem was that couple relationships in the community easily got fused and nondifferentiated. Then the differences between the two people were not seen as differences, but as points of contention. This happened more in lesbian couples than in heterosexual couples, she thought, because of the likeness between women. By choosing a lesbian you were choosing a person with a minimum of differences and so the boundaries were less clear. They were also less clear because these couples did not have rules that had been passed down for generations, that had to do with roles and the emotional division of labor. It was like mirror dancing. People initially picked another person for complementarity in the lesbian community, just as they did in heterosexual relationships. One partner would pick another for a reflection of the opposite to herself: a different body type, for instance, or stability versus a butterfly type, or a different way of dealing with the world.

Then as they got more involved, the relationship would become fused and the differences they picked the other person for would became a negative self-experience. From the fused place, the differences would be felt as threats, because from that place differences were not valued. Oneness was valued. The sense of wholeness and the sense of an ability to survive as a complete person that each person had would become dependent on the fusion of the couple, and people would end up resenting the complementarity they had picked in the beginning. A lot of crazy-making would go on because of this, which made these couples prone to breakups.

What also made them prone to breakups, Kathryn thought, was the fact that the hopes were so high in these relationships: the hopes that, with women relating to women, "We can make it." The stakes were higher here than in male-female relationships because the expectations were so much higher. The self was much more on the line. These were relationships of choice that people made often after having had difficult or unpleasant or unrewarding relationships with men. They were then particularly disappointed, especially with all the ideological pressure that existed, when the relationships turned out to be no different on some levels from other relationships. The instinct was to drop the hot potato at that point because all the understanding and unity that was talked about and expected just wasn't there, and the feelings of loss then were intense.

She had counseled people in the community about this problem of nondifferentiation, but it hadn't changed it. She had tried to give them a better understanding of boundaries and why they needed boundaries. "Fair fighting" was useful sometimes because it provided a way to make the boundaries clear so that the differences could somehow be tolerated, but it didn't challenge the tightness of the basic structure—the fusion. She had tried combinations of things: character work, pointing out inequalities of power, treating couples as part of a network that was the larger community. Many of her ideas came out of work with families: family therapy where there was also this problem of nondifferentiation and not valuing the differences.

After she and Meg started seeing Kathryn, Diana felt, things got to be better in most ways. They were told to set their boundaries, like when a friend of hers asked to put her furniture in their garage. Another person had done this before and Meg had felt invaded. This time they talked with Kathryn and Kathryn said, "Set your boundaries." So she, Diana, said, "Okay, the garage is mine," Meg hooked out and said, "Okay, my space is my study." It became a little more comfortable, though Diana didn't know if Meg entirely hooked out. It was hard to tell with Meg.

Leslie felt she could identify with Meg. Similar things happened with her in her relationship with Gloria. She felt she was a person who just had to have her privacy—her control over her physical environment and her inner soul. Every day she spent time alone. She sought it out especially when she was just flying off the wall. One day a couple of weekends ago, she had gone to the photo lab in the morning. She wanted to hear Meg read poetry at noon. Then Meg's reading was cancelled, so she and Meg and Bronwyn, who Meg was relating to, and Lilith went over to Country Joe's for lunch. They were sitting there talking and Diana walked in with Nell.

Now everyone knew that Diana had threatened Meg with breaking up their relationship if Meg had another affair. So when Diana walked in with Nell, they all just wanted to crawl out, like, "Oh Jesus fucking Christ, what am I supposed to do?" She, Leslie, went over at that point and said hello to Diana. Diana said, "Who are you with?" She said, "Oh, Bronwyn and Meg and Lilith." Diana went white.

Then the four of them—herself, Bronwyn, Meg, and Lilith—went to someone's house afterward to talk about it. They talked about what everyone could do to aid a person. That, for her, was the end of the rope. She had to leave. She was fed up with people. She had to be alone. She came back to her house and Emily was there crying about something else, so she went on a long bike ride. When she came back the second time, Deborah was sitting there crying. Then she went bonkers. She went into her room and slammed the door and smoked marijuana. She couldn't deal with anybody, not even Gloria.

It was like it was a sin to be happy. Everywhere she went in the community, Leslie felt, there were all these crises. She thought that she should maybe help out, give some comfort and hugs and pats. But she didn't want to do that. It was a real struggle to do what she wanted to and not feel like shit and all guilty. When she got to the edge of times like that, like if Gloria and she had a blowup, she wouldn't talk to anyone. Maybe when it was all over she would, but not then. Then she needed to be alone.

She had liked living alone, which was what she had done for two years before she moved in with Gloria. When she moved in with Gloria she had to have her own room. It had taken her a while to feel she was able to have her own space in the house with everyone else around, because Gloria always had people with her and there were also other people living in the house. It took her a while to be able to ask for things. She still found it hard being in the relationship with Gloria and asking for time alone with her. It was easier than before, but still hard because Gloria had needs to be together more of the time. When Gloria was feeling distraught, she wanted to make love. When she, Leslie, was feeling distraught, she wanted to go off by herself. She thought it had to do with backgrounds. Hers was when butt came up against butt, it was herself; there wasn't anybody going to help her. While Gloria was real loving, real Christian, used to being around people.

There were also difficulties concerning times when the two of them would be alone together. She would say to Gloria at the beginning of a day, "I'd like to have some time with you." Then she'd come back later and there would be two or three people invited over for the afternoon. Sometimes the trouble came down to language, like she hadn't specified whether she'd like to be with Gloria with or without other people. That was something that had never happened the other way around.

Gloria, Leslie felt, got things from other people—the group, the community—that she, Leslie, didn't need as much. Gloria was someone who got into the nitty-gritty by talking about jobs and crises and traumas. She sought out a lot of positive feedback from other people and she got it. She sought out people who would be attracted to her sexually but not necessarily make love with her. She sought out people she could get into these incredible ideological discussions with, like about multinational corporations, things that were happening "out there." While she, Leslie, had mainly a few close friends. One was a man and the other two were not in the community.

Gloria agreed that in terms of time to herself, she did not have much need of it. She felt like she was with people from morning to night. Every once in a while it built up and she had to take a morning or an afternoon off, but as a rule she didn't feel the need to. In the past she had been afraid of time to herself. That was why she was moving. She and Leslie were moving to a farm in West Virginia at the end of the summer. She thought the move would help her break this pattern and take more time to herself. Her job as a minister had always had her dealing with people and she wanted to try something new. In addition, she knew that Leslie needed more time alone, more of a sense of privacy.

The problem of time alone versus time with people was, thought Gloria, the most controversial theme in relationships in the community, not only a problem she and Leslie had. The problem was that one person would want to be more private, have more time alone; the other would want to be more public, more social. She thought it began because opposites attracted. They complemented each other. They brought out things in each other that were appreciated. Then the two people had this conflict. She could name couple after couple in the community who had it: Natalie (social) and Jo, Emily (social) and Marla, Chip (social) and Jessica, Ruby (social) and Chandra. Maybe some couples were free of it, she didn't know. Some couples were so new she couldn't tell, like Meg and Bronwyn.

The problem of dealing with the differences, said Kathryn, had to be seen in the context of the fact that these relationships were already under strain because of their being so experimental. They didn't have rules like in heterosexual society, so they had to be experimental, and because they were, it was hard. Sometimes the relationships didn't work, but other times they did work and people didn't recognize it. One area in a relationship wouldn't work and they wouldn't see it as only one area, or they would have a good thing going and then not know when to stop experimenting. They might have a relationship that was fairly peaceful, fairly calm, but then they wouldn't confirm it, they wouldn't validate it. They would always be looking outward. They had this idea that if the relationship was strong, it could take anything, or they thought, "Look what so-and-so's doing. Let's try that," like with nonmonogamy. She, Kathryn, felt she could see it coming when people said they wanted to do such-and-such. She could see that it would break the relationship.

The problem was that the whole community hinged on

incest, thought Bart. It hinged on having close relationships that almost crossed the line of blood. People would put down roots, deep emotional attachments, hopes. It would be that way for six months or a year. And then they'd go off and smatter them.

It mattered to all of them in the community what their group as a unit thought, felt June. She knew of one woman who thought if she made this one move of breaking up with someone, she would be abandoned by the community. That was Gayle who was afraid of splitting up with Lilith. There had been one meeting at the Woman's Center a few weeks ago where Gayle said if she wanted to extricate herself from her relationship with Lilith, she felt she would be abandoned. That meeting told her, June, about what it meant to be connected with this bunch of women, how dependent they were on each other. They seemed to know what was going on with each other real well.

Her fears about leaving Lilith, said Gayle, actually dated from three years ago when she left Natalie. She still didn't really understand it. Three years ago she and Natalie had been seen by everyone as this ideal couple in the community. They were the ones all the young dykes emulated. And they knew they were the perfect couple because every other couple they knew weren't even having sex. At least that was what she thought at the time. She didn't know if Natalie felt the same way. She thought Natalie felt trapped, but they played right into the image. They had a very intense, highly romantic, very private relationship. They didn't talk to anybody in the community about it, the problems in it. They didn't want anyone to know there were problems.

The problems basically had to do with her, Gayle, wanting to be monogamous and Natalie not wanting to be and Natalie telling her everybody felt like Natalie did, and that she, Gayle, would be seen as uptight. Gayle felt humiliated by it and she didn't want anybody to know, so, for her part, she didn't share; she didn't talk. Then it came as a shock to everybody when she left Natalie. People, even the people closest to her, were very angry with her. She tried to talk to them at the time to sort out her thoughts, but she felt they were thinking. "How could she, this monogamous person, do this to Natalie? How could she break up the family?" which was Natalie, herself, Elinor, and Melissa, all of whom were very close. She didn't know how to deal with it. She felt everyone was angry.

So she left Natalie and went to live with Lilith, who was the one person she had been able to talk to. Lilith worked out at Western, the state college where she did, in Queens Crossing. She remembered she said to herself at the time, "You made your bed. Now lie in it." Then she spent the next year and a half in mourning for Natalie. She would wake up every morning crying. Lilith and she spent the year and a half fighting. It was a year and a half more before she finally could admit to herself that she wanted out of the relationship with Lilith, that it had been a mistake to begin with. She had cut herself off from her old friends in the community and she desperately wanted them back. She wanted them to know about how she'd gone through all that time of grieving and self-hate.

While she and Gayle were together, recalled Lilith, the second year they bought a house, Prairie Manor, an old farmhouse on some land halfway between Queens Crossing and town. There was a time for a while after they bought it when things were going well. Then it came as a surprise to her about a year later when Gayle started giving indications that she no longer wanted their relationship and started having an affair with someone else. She, Lilith, had thought she and Gayle had a lifetime commitment to each other, stemming from their feelings about their previous breakups where they had both left a primary person (Gayle had left Natalie and she, Lilith, had broken up with Jo, who then went to live with Natalie). Things got gradually worse between her and Gayle until it got to a point where if and when Gayle came home to Prairie Manor, Gayle would ignore her existence. Or Gayle would act crazy, for example, turning the record player way up and lying on the couch and not coming upstairs, and they had earphones. When this began to happen, Lilith asked that Gayle take her cats and not show up for another month. She also started talking with people at that point and they counseled her to start doing self-care so that no matter what Gayle did, she would be okay.

Since then, which was about three weeks ago, Lilith hadn't known what Gayle was doing. She didn't see Gayle much. Gayle was seeking support from a whole other set of people, people who didn't know the history. People Lilith was talking to were advising her to accept it. They had volunteered ritual crying time, raging time, and that sort of thing. When Gayle came out to Prairie Manor to get her things, there were people right there willing to have dinner with Lilith, to take her out.

It was difficult, however, Lilith felt, because she sensed that people were wanting her to accept the breakup faster than she was willing to accept it. She also wondered how long they would put up with her being a melancholy mess. People like Natalie would say: "Yeah, these are the same problems I had with Gayle. Be happy they're over. You will soon be grateful." It was helpful to get the perspectives of people, Lilith thought. It took her out of the craziness she felt with Gayle, but part of her wanted to feel like she did without constraints: to be angry and miserable, to not keep her commitments.

Francis was now staying with her out at Prairie Manor for a while and that also helped, since Francis was having to recover from her relationship with Diana. Francis had been relating to Diana. Then, as of last Friday night, Diana had started to get back together with Meg, so all the commitments Diana had made to Francis had gone totally out the window and Francis was now feeling what Lilith had been feeling. Francis hadn't been totally understanding until then. It was not a cognitive understanding that mattered, Lilith felt, it was a gut-level understanding, that they knew: it was like someone dying on you.

She'd had similar feelings in her breakup with Lucy, recalled Alice. She had talked with Lilith at the time. Lilith had volunteered to act as a mediator between her and Lucy. She helped them set up a period of separation so they could cool down and decide what to do. Other people in the community offered things as well, people who didn't even know her well. They told her, Alice, about self-care: that there were some practical, simple ways for her to handle things so she could have some control. They gave her insights she thought if she'd had before, the breakup might not have happened. People said she could stay at their house. If she called them, they would talk with her. If they didn't hear from her for a day or so, they would call to make sure she was okay. They were allies at parties: they would sit with her or leave with her if Lucy came in with her new lover Rhonda. Finally, though, she felt she was boring them all and that she was still too overwhelmed by her feelings, so she had to withdraw.

She'd had an experience like that too, said Sarah, when Helen started pulling back from their relationship. Something changed between her and the community then. Whereas before she hadn't talked to people about how she felt in relation to Helen, because she wouldn't want to acknowledge it, now she wanted people to see her as having had something important invested with Helen. She wanted them to help her keep it, and she thought they did, primarily by relating to her as an individual they even liked, so she could feel whole alone.

She had talked with people in the community more than she ever had before during that period when Helen was drawing back, and she felt they came to know intimate facts of her personal life. As a result she felt very exposed. At the same time she felt more part of the community than ever before. She felt protected by it. At one party at Marla's, Lilith came up to where she was sitting watching Helen and Lilith said she could see she was looking with longing.

She was impressed with their efforts, said Kathryn, their intense, persistent efforts at loving, at friendships, their efforts not to lose people. Even when you were breaking up, they knew, you were still on the same side of the fence. These relationships were hard, she felt. The community tried to use everything it possibly could to solve the problems. The differentiation issue was central. The community or the couple became this ego mass.

The main problems were the lack of differentiation and the fusion which led to some of the crazy-making, and the intense disappointment when the relationships broke up or weren't as different or as perfect as people expected they would be.

When Alice was going through her problems breaking up with Lucy, Chip recalled, she and Jessica had helped her. They had a desire to help her with some things they were also going through at the time. They had a desire to share what they knew. That was how it was in this community, she felt: people had a stake in each other's feelings.

8

A Subgroup

She thought, said Hollis, that people in the community privately interacted with each other on the basis of their familiarity and years together. They had intense interactions that tended to go on behind the scenes in groups or in private homes and friendships. There were certain people involved, she couldn't call them charismatic characters, but they were certainly powerful characters. They were the people who ran things like the newsletter; they owned the homes in which the parties took place; they had cars so they could travel places; they organized the Arts Festival. Their power resided in their material resources and in the length of time they had been here. If you had stayed here and bought a house and had a job here and were older (upwards of twenty-five), it definitely gave you status in the community. She had heard this said many times.

The Thursday night support group Natalie was in was central to the whole thing known as the community, felt Nikki. That group at some point took up more space than it had a right to. It held itself up as a giant. For a long time the people in that group were the only ones in the area who were articulate as lesbians. Other people came in later, but the people in that group already had seniority. They claimed to be the most political and revolutionary, but they really stood for middle-class values. They valued the ability to speak in front of groups. They valued assertiveness. They had this real Hollywood air about them, an air that implied that there were some perfect women. Being among them was like walking down a hall of portraits with people who were outstanding in it; it just sort of ignored most of the people in this world. The women in that group valued intelligence, not pedantic intelligence and not intense intelligence, but a kind of bright sorority-type intelligence. They valued a certain amount of social standing and material comfort.

She had a theory, said Lucy, about why that particular support group existed and why she didn't think it was healthy. She thought some people became so extremely dependent on the kind of feedback they got from certain other people, and this feedback became so important in their socializing, that other people outside that small group couldn't fulfill whatever it was they needed and it got to be inbred. It was almost as if a new language would begin to develop, a new set of communication.

The main reason she felt this was back a few years ago she had been involved in this group when it was still a suport group for the Women's Shelter. She had felt the closedness of the group increase quickly and to such a great extent at that time. Along with that closedness, there developed a set of ideas that these people embraced. If you did not embrace those ideas, if you were not part of that group, you became an outsider when any number of them would gather.

She had left the group at the start of the summer after it broke away from the Women's Shelter. She was thinking of going back in the fall, but by the time the fall came, she felt the group had turned into a monster. There was an acceptable versus an unacceptable way to think and do things. There were definite leaders in the group who had to be listened to above all else, although it was supposed to be a leaderless group. Certain people would say, "This is what I want the group to be," and that was what the group would be. Natalie, especially, would do that. She was not afraid to say what she wanted and to say it in a way that was not offensive to people, and other people respected that, or just blindly followed.

There were other leaders too, like Ruby and Elinor, though there were also people like Marla who always stated things that were unpopular. People would give Marla a hard time, but she would hold her ground. Marla was one of the few people who got into that scene and always held her own thoughts.

There was, she knew, resentment against the Thursday night support group she was in, said Gloria. There was resentment against both Thursday night groups. People in the broader community resented these groups because the people in them were educated, professional, radical, and separatist. She had heard this said at the last coffeehouse that was held as a community meeting in the winter. It was clear that certain people in the community perceived these groups as having all the power in the community and that they perceived themselves as outsiders.

She thought that people in the groups, however, would say, "No, there are no 'ins' and 'outs,' we are all in this together." The people who perceived that they didn't have the power defined themselves as an outgroup, she felt. They didn't participate and consequently they didn't take the power. For example, they didn't volunteer to put out the newsletter or run the coffeehouse, and that wasn't a consequence of what the Thursday night groups were doing, but of what they were not doing.

At the same time, that meeting had made her think about how those of them in the Thursday night groups needed to be more careful, like about making information known that there would be a Womanspirit Celebration or a May Day or a Seder. They had to be very careful about not defining the community so narrowly as to exclude people who might want in. That was difficult, though, because there would be people you might want to reach out to who might slap your hand: people who might have recently decided they were lesbians, for example, and then would be horrified if you mentioned it.

It was also hard because of how things developed, like the first year the May Day and the Seder were closed rituals. They were mainly for members of the two Thursday night groups, unless you had a significant other you wanted to bring and you let the group know in advance. That was partly because, in the beginning, when members of the groups had experimented with some of the first rituals, they held them open and a few of the women who came were hostile and hissed and giggled and it made them all uncomfortable. They therefore decided to keep the May Day and the Seder closed that first year. Then this year when people in the groups were more comfortable with the whole idea of rituals and more familiar with them, they opened them up. But they still said that only those who weren't going to be hostile should come.

The people in the Thursday night groups, she felt, had an ethic: you had to ask for what you wanted, you were responsible for yourself. All along the people in the groups had been about getting what they wanted. They had assumed other people would do the same. That was part of the problem. It was also partly a class thing. It was very easy to get the college-educated, middle-class, professional women together and feeling they had the corner on the revolution. Because of this, what the other women were saying at that meeting was very important for her to hear—that they and others were feeling excluded and that the groups needed to make some intentional efforts to open things up.

There would still be some kinds of activities however, that she would prefer to keep private. In her own group she felt that, as a group, in some ways they were pushing their limits. They were not sure what would happen. Like now they were talking in the group about sexuality among group members. They were trying to deal with it more openly because the sense of identification of people in the group was increasingly not in couples but in communty. Last Thursday night, for instance, they had talked in the group about group sex, like everybody making love to one person as a group activity. (That had started with a discussion of people's feelings about the kissing ritual they'd had on May Day.) Group sex was now just a big fantasy, but everybody was sitting down and talking about it and thinking about what it meant. It was a big de-privatizing step within the group, and it wasn't the kind of thing to open up to the larger community.

She liked the fact that certain things were kept only within that group, said Marla. She liked the sense in the group of having a real private experience with those people and not having it taken outside. They'd had a confidentiality code in the group since the start which had even applied to not talking to each other between meetings. It had to do with building trust in the group so people could feel safe. At first the code was strict. Then it was loosened up so you could talk to significant others. She had liked the code being tight though. She liked it not because it was privacy, but because it was bond. The bond kept the information people brought to the group within the group so their experience didn't get diluted.

There were very few things that went on in the lives of members of that group that they didn't tell each other, felt Harriet. They'd been meeting together every week for four and a half years, the same eight of them; though in some periods people came and went. The people in that group, she felt, were all very committed to each other. She also felt that she was in a group, as different from being in "the core" or "the core of the core," as some people in the community called it. She felt that there were people in her group who were committed to the development of a community in their own self-interests and that they knew they were only going to make that happen if there was a larger group of people who would support them in living. The people in the group needed the people outside, the ones who felt they were being excluded, in order to build a community.

Those in the group who were most committed to building a community, she felt, were Marla, Natalie, Ruby, and maybe Helen, although with Helen it was on another level because if Helen got a job somewhere else, she would probably move. While other people, like Natalie and Ruby, were committed to the geographic area, in part because they had tenure. In addition to that, the people in the group were very similar in many ways. Almost everybody made money by teaching: Natalie, Ruby, Stacy, Ellen, herself—she taught part-time. Helen was tied to education, as was Marla; Gayle used to teach; Gloria was a minister. They consequently shared a focus on the way people thought and how they learned.

The group members were also similar in age. Their ages ranged from twenty-eight (Stacy) to thirty-six or thirty-seven (Natalie), which was ten years and it was an interesting ten years in the whole culture. And this was the freak generation.

Their incomes also weren't very widely spread. All of the people in the group were fairly comfortable. Marla was poorer now because she was a student. Helen was a student too and her income was lower, but in some ways it wasn't because she had child support. Ruby and Natalie made good incomes from teaching at Marshall. Her own income and Stacy's were close to theirs. When these people were in school they had all gotten good grades. They were all achievers. No dummies in this group.

There were differences in their class backgrounds, however. Natalie, Gloria, and Gayle were middle class. Marla, herself, and Ruby came from lower-class backgrounds. Natalie she was not sure about. They had done a lot of talking in the group about class background and how it affected things like their families' different ideas of what a large present was had recently created some discomfort for Marla. Their religious backgrounds were also real varied. She, Harriet, was Congregational; Stacy, Marla, and Helen were Jewish; Ruby was Catholic; Natalie, Southern Methodist; Gloria was Protestant; Ellen was Protestant, almost Catholic. At the Seder this year six out of twenty-seven were Jews. It was organized by Marla. The religious backgrounds made for a non-common experience which caused some disagreement when it came to the development of rituals. Natalie, for example, thought of what they were doing in the community as building a new religion with the rituals; whereas someone like Gloria said no, they had to put new meaning back in the old religion. There was that kind of difference.

But members of the group differed most, Harriet felt, in how they conducted relationships. Goals ran from monogamy all the way through to polygamy. (Natalie was actually talking about multiple committed relationships; it was more than non-monogamy.) Also, there was a scale that ran from romance to nonromance. Natalie was all the way over on one side of both scales. She believed in cold, calculating polygamous relationships. She used romance to get into sexual moods, but she would not order her life according to some romantic love, while people like Gloria and Helen would. There was, in addition, a certain amount of pressure on the romantic people in the group to become nonromantic. This pressure was implied by people's responses to other people's problems, like, "Oh my God, I can't stand it," or "When are you going to get control of your life?" "Shut up," or other nonsympathetic statements.

The way people in the group conducted their relationships was a more primary difference between them than class background or religion, Harriet felt. Sometimes the way the members of the group conducted their relationships affected how much privacy they sought. Romantic people who got swept away by passion were likely to get involved with other people who were swept away by passion, and these people were always saying, "I slept with so-and-so, but DON'T TELL ANYONE," though of course they would tell the group. People in the group generally could be rated according to the different levels of privacy they sought for their relationships. They ran all the way from Ellen who told the least, to Ruby and Natalie, possibly, who had this great love of gossip.

After four or five years in that group, felt Ruby, she knew everybody's privacy needs. She knew who you didn't walk in on when they were going to the bathroom, who could make love in front of you, who wanted to make love without anybody around, who didn't care if you heard 'em, who didn't care if you heard and saw 'em, who didn't care if you participated, who needed time to meditate alone, who needed time to themselves every day.

The people in that group were very close. Their closeness came from their talking, from their sharing, from their ritualizing ways of getting through difficult emotional times, like through use of fair fighting. Though sometimes she, Ruby, did feel that her psychic space had been violated in the group or that she had lost a sense of herself. She thought that came when someone had blabbed too much or when she had blabbed, when that happened and either she or the other person was too close to the experience. Recently, for example, when she saw a sister ignoring a primary relationship and focusing all her energy on a love affair, she had thought that she probably confused some of her own frustration about working on relationships with what this sister was telling her, which caused her to become angry. She didn't realize that until later, however, when she described the event to others.

Her own pattern, recalled Helen, had been to be in and out of the group over the years. She had started meeting with them at the Women's Shelter. Then she didn't meet with them for two semesters during her first year back in school. She started meeting with them again when the group started taking a more personal turn and things began getting bad between her and Meg so that she wanted to talk about it. She had been meeting with them when her health started going down the tubes and she was being checked for blood cancer. The group was very supportive. They took care of her the week she was blind. They stayed with her; they took over her kids. She had more of an involvement in the group from then on. She had felt closer to them as a result of their support during her illness, and that feeling of closeness continued to this day.

She felt, however, that she was one of the lessverbal people in that group, especially when the discussion got political. But she felt she learned a lot from the women in there—about how people behaved, about how she behaved. For example, she had learned a lot about self-care and she had learned about how different everyone's perceptions were. That was what amazed her. In a lot of ways she felt the group mirrored the greater society, except that the people in it happened to be more verbal.

They talked a lot in that group, felt Jessica. She had been involved with it back in the beginning. She wasn't part of it now (she was in the other Thursday night group), but there was a time when she had kind of forced herself in. She had matched them for a while. She was real outspoken and pushy, talking about whatever they talked about. She went ahead and joined them even when they weren't wanting outsiders, and something happened to her during that time: some kind of growth. There was also a sense of vulnerability that she got. She had never figured it out. She still felt it with those people, except for Helen. She thought it had to do with the fact that the people in that group, if they had feelings, they put them in words and it became inhuman. She had felt this way then. She also felt she didn't have the same sort of background as the rest of them: she wasn't college-educated, she wasn't from a home where she had been taught how to speak. But she had joined them because she wanted to be part of it. She just wanted to be part of those women.

Her experience with that group, recalled Chandra, the "core of the core," was a lot through Ruby. She had drawn back from it. She didn't think basically she trusted the people in that group, and consequently they didn't trust her. Her experience with them, however, had helped her be more articulate and clear about herself, about what she liked and did not like, how she preferred to spend her time, who she was.

She had been involved since the old days at the Women's Shelter, said Stacy. At first she didn't talk about her relationships with men, her sexual relationships. Then after the group broke away from the Shelter, she began to feel close enough with the women so she could talk about anything she wanted to. Now she felt that the pressure against talking about her relationships with men came from women outside, not from the group. It came from people she didn't know as well. She felt that people in the group really knew her and that they thought of her generally as a healthy type of person. They felt that her relationship with her husband was what she had chosen. It was not like relationships some women in the community had with men where they were wanting to get out.

Harriet, who was her friend and who was also a straight woman in the group, had recently started having an affair with a woman and had talked about it in the group. Harriet was initially concerned that she, Stacy, would be upset because she was the last one left, like being the last teenager to drink or the last anybody to do anything. Harriet thought she might almost quit because of that, but she, Stacy, felt that her experience in the group was pretty much the same as it had always been. Maybe she felt twinges, like a feeling that her life style was being abandoned or that everybody would say "We've only got one left," but she felt these pressures were mostly made up. They were not there on the outside.

With Harriet in the group, there was a kind of balance that she didn't think would change just because of Harriet's affair. It was not a battle, but in terms of consciousness and certain casual remarks, it helped that there were two of them. She, Stacy, then wouldn't feel she always had to be the one to say "Hey, that hurts." There had always been a lot of reassurance from other people in the group that "the word 'dyke' is meant to include you as well." Nonetheless she had felt some ambivalence—that she wanted to be included, but it was also excluding a lot that she was. There were simply these dilemmas.

If they took this step of having a sexual ritual for closeness with the group, for instance, she would probably go along, even if it was something she didn't particularly want to do. She would take part because of wanting to feel the closeness and because it was not necessarily objectionable just because it wasn't something she wanted. If she went along, people would see that although she wasn't an active lesbian, she wanted to feel part of the group. She would do it as a bonding thing. She knew she didn't have to, but she would certainly feel more isolated by choosing not to. She felt a lot of the women in the group had the same fears. She didn't think she had them any more than the others just because she hadn't been sexual with another woman. She did think, however, that the others were wanting to see just what her reaction was going to be.

This group was very important to her. From the start, her main attraction to the community had been that, though she chose not to relate sexually to women, women who were lesbian were most attractive to her. They were attractive in terms of being physical with each other, being open with each other, being caring and committed to each other. That was hard to find outside of a lesbian community. There were moderate-type feminists outside, but they were more interested in passing the ERA and less interested in each other. She, Stacy, thought that if ever she moved to a new place, she would go to the women's center and say she was looking for a lesbian group that had non-lesbian women in it.

It was only recently, said Jill, that she'd understood what the Thursday night groups really were, that there was a myth and a reality. The myth was that they were several elite groups that got together and talked about what was relevant for them and that they were very powerful in the community and very choosy about who was included. The reality was that they were just support groups. She had been in one since the fall, the group Lilith and Gayle had formed.

She had been in a couple of support groups in the community, noted Ruth, not the core Thursday night group, but a couple of others. A lot of intimate things had come up and she had found she wasn't comfortable. Maybe she was just being defensive, but she didn't think really intimate things were best discussed in an arena of six or eight people. She didn't know. Sometimes she thought it would be nice to be able to be intimate like that, to let people know her that way, but it was not something she had been able to do. For her, it happened more by having certain friends. Things that were really important to her—her life desires, her ambitions, her dreams—she only talked about with a few people.

She had this fear, said Cheryl, that kept her from being involved. She had been involved in groups before and she got burnt out. She could, she supposed, maintain a supportive relationship with different individual women in the community, but getting too involved, like getting more involved in a group, did not appeal to her. She felt she would lose herself.

She thought, said Kelly, that she hadn't gotten more involved in groups in the community because she didn't know them. It was also because she didn't want people knowing too much about her, probably because she didn't know it herself. She could see getting caught up real easily if she were to participate more. She had, however, joined the consort that played with the choir. The people in it were outsiders like herself. Nikki called her one day and she wasn't really interested, but she thought she would do it anyway to see what it was like and because she hadn't played her flute in eight years.

She thought, said Martha, that the wider community had begun to adopt a small group structure. That seemed to be the only way to go. She was thinking of the new support groups that had started and the consort and the choir and the teams.

There was a certain cliquishness about the community now, felt Judith. Several years ago when the community was smaller, she used to see more of some people than she did now. There were mainly the parties that would bring them together. They had to make do; so whether the parties were where you wanted to be or not, you went. Now, however, there was more space for choosing. There were more numbers, more groups. The subgroups she was in were volleyball, basketball, and the choir. She thought that within their small groups people might be more open now than they had been in the past in the larger community, though she didn't really know.

She did not, said Helen, think that the Thursday night group she was in was the power group in the community, or that there was one power person in that group. She knew Natalie had certainly been outspoken and people thought of her as powerful

(Natalie seemed to have a tremendous amount of charisma), but mainly Natalie was bright and even. She was fair. Their Thursday night group was seen as the core, Helen felt, because it represented a kind of cohesion that didn't exist anywhere else in the community in a larger bonding than two. Also, it had been around for a long time, four and a half years.

She had known right away, said Emily, that there was a core Thursday night group and that the people in it were the heavies in this community, but she didn't have any resentment. She saw Natalie instantly as the chief dyke of the community. Natalie was the center because she was the center of that group, and also because she was highly verbal, charismatic, physically powerful, intense, took charge, was real honest and straightforward about what she was going to do, had been here longer than a lot of the women, was a property owner and a professional, was perceived as having a lot of power and seen as the ideal dyke by a lot of women who were not in the in-crowd.

Who was the ideal dyke? The ideal dyke had a lot of friends. She, Emily, had thought at first that Natalie had a lot of affairs, that everyone wanted to be sexual with her—young dykes, baby dykes, they would all come pay homage to Natalie. The ideal dyke was real popular, she had her health, she was physically attractive, real sensual, sexual, independent, strong, dramatic.

She knew, said Natalie, that the Thursday night groups were seen as powerful in the community. These groups were considered powerful by people who didn't have friends yet. Newer people felt this, but what they were thinking of as power was really synonymous with comfort. It was standing around at a party talking with friends, as opposed to being an outsider, a newcomer. The accusation of elitism, what people saw as elitism in the community, was primarily the result of living in one place for a long time. Early in the genesis of the community, there were women who were perceived as having power: those who were older and more articulate, meaning they spoke the most. However that was diminishing now because of community and radical feminist norms of equality. Talkers like herself were trying to be real disciplined about controlling things.

Because she was physically big, tall, and verbal, she had been seen as a center of the community, Natalie thought. But she was seen as more of a center than she was. She did not see herself as charismatic. In fact, she resisted that. She saw herself as one of a handful of true believers. She felt she had made a conscious decision not to pursue fame. Nonetheless, she had always been a sociable person. Her rewards had always come from people. She enjoyed it that way, though sometimes she felt she was spreading herself too thin, and sometimes she had delusions of grandeur. She would feel that if she didn't do something, no one else would. She had felt like this since she was young. She also thought she was seen as central for a lot of accidental reasons.

Sometimes in the community she would sense a kind of surprise in dealing with people face to face—that people were surprised to be having a normal interaction with her. She felt resented by a few people in the community because she was comfortable and had friends when they didn't. She could recall at least three occasions with three different people where they had come up to her at a party and said sarcastically at the end, "Oh, another evening of good conversation." She checked with them later and it turned out they had wanted to talk with her and she hadn't come over and talked to them, so they were blaming her for it.

She thought that had to do with her publicness, with what they expected her to be, because in actuality she was shy with people and not in the habit of talking one to one very often. In actual relationships, in her support group and with people she was close to, she felt she was perceived as an equal, a peer.

Natalie had been labeled the superstar, said Kathryn, and she acted like she didn't know it was happening and, on the other hand, like that was where she was supposed to be.

There were certain people in the community who were not called leaders, noted Francis, but in reality they were perceived as leaders. She had been introduced into the community by one of these people—Natalie—so it had been easier for her to become involved than if she had started on the fringes. She was then adopted by women who were involved in the so-called elite group, which she had thought was perfectly hilarious, because her perception of them was that they were not elitist at all. She saw them as being energetic, creative, and, to her, very inclusive, but then that was where her own sense of privacy came in—in that she felt they were entitled to the privacy of their support group. She had been totally washed away when she heard all the claims about there being these exclusive Thursday night groups because it had never occurred to her that she had any right to know what went on in those groups. It simply didn't occur. She thought if they wanted to have rituals of their own, okay.

9

Coming and Going

She left the community three years ago and moved to a farm, said Aurora. She had been involved with the Women's Shelter before she left—with the personal support group there—and had burned out with the personal relationships, so she was really looking forward to the privacy and aloneness the farm was offering. She was just coming back into the community now after being away and in some ways she was feeling like a stranger. She was feeling it awkward to relate to all these people she had once related to quite closely.

Back when she had left, she was doing a lot: going to support group meetings at the Women's Shelter, helping with the different committees and doing odd jobs, going out to eat or just being with a lot of the people, feeling really close to them. She was feeling very relaxed with the different people. Then they had this retreat at Bart's farm with the Women's Shelter group where she started having this affair with a woman who was straight and a feminist with the Shelter. She felt a lot of guilt. There were other women who she knew were interested in this woman and had tried to approach her and she had said no. These people were kind of hurt. She, Aurora, knew this because of cues, like their putting a head trip on her—like what was Mary, her lover, going to feel? So she fled the whole situation, to get away from everybody and to run from the guilt, she supposed.

After that it was easy to stop seeing people from the community when she moved to the farm. It was a long trip for them to come out there. (For people in this town twenty minutes was a long trip.)

She moved to the farm with Mary. She and Mary withdrew from the community and the more they withdrew, the more isolated they began to feel. The community, the town they moved to, where Mary's parents had some land, was a very Christian community and it was easy to slip into the ideas of that community. It was fairly easy to flip-flop and leave the lesbian community and get into the spirit of the German Lutheran community. You went to Sunday School and you were suddenly part of it. The community out there became all they really needed, particularly once Mary and she decided they'd go straight, which meant celibate for herself, straight for Mary. That was after about a year. Then they weren't hiding anything. It, the past, being lesbian, was nothing.

Before they moved to the farm, she, Aurora, had always felt very threatened by her parents coming to town, because then she and Mary would have to take down all the cards and hide the books to get ready for the visit. On the farm, however, it was more relaxed, they didn't have to do any of that because they weren't lesbian anymore. It was a relief. It was also boring, but at the time it was what she wanted.

The religion was very important. Because she and Mary weren't relating to anyone in the lesbian community, they withdrew more and more into the ideas of the people around them. Her own parents were of the same denomination and lived in a small town nearby and it was like going home to go to church with them. It gave her parents a lot of support and they were thrilled. That all lasted for about a year to a year and a half. Then Mary started to date men. When that happened, she, Aurora, knew she wasn't straight. She was definitely gay and she was really missing the closeness and the feelings of intimacy that Mary and she had shared. The whole thing threw her. She started seeing a counselor at the time—Ruby from the community—and once again she felt support for being gay and for other things as well. Ruby started asking her to think about what kind of commitment she wanted from Mary. She was wanting to be gay again with Mary. When she told Mary that, Mary said she would be her friend for life. That lasted for about three months, because she, Aurora, didn't want a roommate. She wanted a woman she could really relate with, not a woman who was dating.

After that she looked for an apartment in town and moved back in the winter. She chucked fundamentalist Christianity. It was pretty much a mind game to a lesbian. She had been identifying with the people at the time she got into it because she had been looking for a community then. Since she had fled the community here, she had needed something to replace it. When she was growing up, she had been part of a community too: the small town about thirty miles from here where her parents still lived, the small town and the fundamentalist church. Her moving to the farm and that whole way of life was just like going back to her childhood, totally.

Then when she decided to move back to town, it was definitely with the lesbian community in mind. She had been keeping in touch with Ruby, who was still counseling her pretty heavily. In the fall she had come to grips with the fact that she was gay and that she wanted to live intimately with another woman. Then in February, soon after she moved back, she started getting to know Roxanne whom she'd had for a class at Marshall, the community college. She went to the Valentine's dance at one of the coffeehouses in the church, and after that she gradually started doing things again with different people. She started seeing individual people and getting in touch with some key people from her past. She went to events. She joined the choir, not only because she liked to sing, but because she was feeling it was hard to get back into this community. She was feeling on the outskirts and wanting to step back in quickly.

At the same time, she was really reluctant at first to talk with people about what had happened since she'd left. It had been really painful; the whole process with Mary had been painful. She also felt real funny about how people in the community were going to react. She thought people would think she had changed a lot. What was more, Roxanne had just broken up with her lover of seven years and she, Aurora, did not know how people would react to that.

People hadn't asked many questions of her, which puzzled her. She had been real curious too, because she wondered how much of what she felt they thought was just conjecture on her part. They may have simply assumed she had been out of town. It was one thing not to give out information, she found, but then you didn't get any, either. When she came back, it was like she had been in Alaska, in more ways than one.

After a while, though, she came to feel that maybe she needed the time, even if it's being slow was hard. She needed the time to get back in and relate to people individually and to feel more secure, because at first when people would say, "Where were you?" she would clutch in fear of their reactions. So she took steps gradually, one at a time, like going to the Memorial Day picnic, helping Ruby move, and going to the Texas Day party. The Texas Day party was relaxed. It was also strange. At that party she was sitting and chatting with a woman she knew from before. She told this woman that Mary had gone straight and this woman said, "I just heard the other day she was going with another woman." She, Aurora, went, "Oh, no," and collapsed, but then she thought maybe Mary was going back to relating to her true sexuality. It was hard to understand it, this skipping back and forth.

She had only recently been coming into town again and seeing people, said Anna. Only this past fall had she started breaking out of her hermit pattern. She had lived in town for four or five years before; then her hermit time had been about four or five years. Before her hermit period, she was not a lesbian until right at the end. Then she met her first lover, Becky, and they moved out to the farm. Three months later, Becky split to Oregon and left her as a hermit out there. That was five years ago. She, Anna, stayed on the farm by herself after that. She didn't feel much like moving out. She was pretty lonely, but she had a social misfit dog. It would have been hard to move into town with a social misfit dog.

Out on the farm her nearest neighbor was a third of a mile away. She didn't feel confined like she did here in town, where you couldn't walk in front of an open window nude because the neighbors would see. Out there, there was no pressure on what you could do. There was a kind of hermit's privacy. If you were all by yourself, no one could interfere with you.

She used to think of her house as a cave at first when she was living there. That was where her hermit identity started, though she was dropping that identity a little now. She'd had a few years of seeing a shrink and she was feeling a lot better about herself, so she could take people more. She hadn't been able to tolerate them in her space for quite a while. She would just feel uncomfortable, fearful of people a lot, fearful of having them in her space. She was reading things into their reactions, sort of seeing herself in their eyes. She had her own vision of herself and she was thinking they were seeing her that way and she didn't like that happening.

She did see other people from time to time during her hermit period, but those were mostly people who were straight, from the faculty at Southern, the state college where she taught. They were into family and kids. She didn't know many people up here to speak of, except for Diana who also taught at Southern. Diana used to live in the farmhouse before she and Becky moved in.

Then this past fall, she, Anna, just had a feeling that she was ready and she wanted to do it, she wanted to come back. She knew Diana was going to be around, so at least she'd know one person in the room. (Diana had been gone for a year, the last time she split with Meg.) This fall, then, she began coming out of her hermit state. She went to one of the coffeehouses. It took a little effort to get in through the door, but then she had a good time. She talked with Mitzi. Then Mitzi invited her to Thanksgiving at Natalie's. Generally she did all right after that, except for one time at Diana's, at Diana and Meg's game party, when she had to leave. She had come in a fearful mood. At one point she was almost crying. Diana thought it was something that had to do with her, Diana's, mood at the time, since she was going through some kind of conflict. Maybe Diana could have pulled her out of it, Anna thought, but she really didn't know anyone at that party, so she left after about an hour.

Then after that she felt she just had to pick herself up and dive back in. Other than at that one party, she felt she had mostly good experiences, talking to everyone. There were so many interesting people. Five or six years ago she had started going to meetings in the community. Maybe there were five or six people at them and she wouldn't feel they had much in common. All that group could do was sit around and talk about being lesbians. But in this group now there was always someone who was willing to talk about just about anything you wanted to get into, except astronomy. She felt a lot better, like at that Texas party, that was the first time she had felt relaxed in a group of people in years. There was ninety percent relaxation and ten percent tension. The other times were fifty-fifty.

She still didn't know people that well, though, even after seven or eight months. She'd heard about the fast grapevines around, but it didn't bother her, unless people would be saying evil things. The only thing that would bother her, she felt, would be if she got misinterpreted and everybody judged that she had done something wrong.

Right now what she was feeling mainly was impatience. She had wanted to dive in and be a full member of the group in one hour, but she knew that was impossible and in a way she didn't want it to happen too fast. She wanted to observe first and find out what was going on. Different people, since she'd been coming back into town, had been easier to get to know. She had always wanted for somebody to come up and talk to her, so that had been a little difficult, but for the most part people had extended enough so she felt she could talk with them, or get going on it. After a while she was going to need to get back to her farm though. She wanted to be in and be closer, but she also wanted to keep the farm as a refuge. She felt she still needed a limit on how long she could be with people.

She had strong feelings about things political, said Pat, but she didn't usually voice them. Then about a year ago this time a letter came out in the community newsletter about the Westover Music Festival in Michigan and she wrote a letter back. Her letter was critical of the attitude she felt women had in this community, which was reflected in the letter she had read in the newsletter. After that all hell broke loose. That was when she withdrew from the community. She was also having difficulties with her relationship at the time. She went into her apartment and locked herself in and didn't have anything to do with anybody.

She just concentrated on her work, which she dearly loved (she was a member of the town police force), and athletics, which she also loved, and didn't have anything to do with the lesbian community for a year. She felt what she did was to make a full circle from when she had first come out: from being totally open to being totally closed. She sort of saw the community as this push-and-pull thing, this double standard: "We love you if you agree with us, if you don't cause us any flack."

She only found out later that some people had agreed with what she had said in her letter and, even if they disagreed, had agreed with her right to say it. She realized now that lesbians in this community were human beings, but it had taken her a year to come to that. She had stepped into the bar again for the first time only about a month ago.

What happened was that after her letter came out in the

newsletter, she got five letters in response: three from one person in the community and two letters from another. These were not letters to the newsletter but personal letters to her home. She tried answering them, but the people kept writing back disagreeing. She also got a couple of phone calls. It was about seven or eight little things, which wasn't much, but it wrecked up her idea of support and nurturing. She had tried in her letter to the newsletter to make a statement that was apersonal, but in their responses these people acted like it was a personal attack, and these were central people in the community. Their personal things were probably threatened, she felt, their barbecues and their dancing under the moon. She wrote back to them restating her position and just kept getting these really vicious letters in return, and that wasn't what she had wanted. She had written her letter to the newsletter to state another view. Then people thought she totally disagreed with them, which wasn't true.

The general reaction was far more negative than she would ever have expected. People attacked her; they attacked her job. It got to a point where her carrying a gun was attacked, intimating, of course, that she misused it. She had never misused it. It sat in her holster and rusted. They said, "What do you know about oppression? You're the oppressor."

In her original letter to the newsletter, she had made it a point to sign her name so everyone would know she wrote it, but she didn't sign her last name or mention the Force. She didn't think that mattered. What she said was immediately associated with the fact that she was a police officer however. She didn't harass people, but still she wasn't taken on her merits. She thought this was because people were so shocked that someone had disagreed with them. No one had disagreed with them this way before, at least not in their own ranks. The phone calls she got were a little toned down from the letters, maybe because it was harder to speak directly to somebody and be so vicious toward them. They didn't refer to her job on the phone. It would have been really difficult to say "You're the oppressor, you carry a gun" on the phone. She thought also that if she had talked to these people face to face, it would have made a difference, but she just didn't have the energy at the time.

When she first wrote her letter, she had felt that the direction of the movement in this town was becoming basically superficial. That was about all she had wanted to say. At about that time awful things were happening. A lesbian was shot and killed, a woman who was not in the community. This woman and her lover had been to the bar. One day the woman's ex-husband came over and shot her twice in the head and killed her. She, Pat, thought that if that had been one of the women of the community, if it had been one of their friends, the roof would have come off this town.

The incident made the papers. It happened last year just before the Westover Music Festival. She had thought people in the community would have been saddened by it, but nothing was said. She would have written her letter, she believed, even if she had not been a police officer. As it was, she had to work the case. She was the first officer on the scene. Her job had given her some raw insights into life, she felt, which she didn't think most people had, and these insights had increased the depth of feeling in her letter.

She withdrew from the community more or less after the responses she got. Before she had gone to parties, she had gone to coffeehouses. She hadn't been actively involved in the political superstructure of the community, if there was one, or the weekly meetings, because of the double standard: they had to vote you in. To her it reeked of sororities. She stopped going to the bar in the summer, but she continued her athletics, although a lot of her athletics went from team-oriented to individual-oriented. They went from team-oriented with lesbians, to playing racketball with straight people, playing basketball with straight people, and swimming and running by herself. That pattern was a real relief for her and it was still more or less how her athletics were. Like this year she was playing on a softball team which was outwardly straight but had some gay members. Right now that was about how she felt about wanting to get back into the community and staying away at the same time. It was a good transition.

When she first became involved in the community, recalled Camille, she was active in the gay organization at the university and was going to the bar. That was nearly three years ago. It was a period of her having crushes on people, activism and crushes. In the spring of that year she used some people—two gay women and one straight man. She used them sexually, she felt, without really knowing what she was doing. She slept with one of the women and then the other on the same weekend and somewhat misled the man. The three of them talked about it and confronted her, and then she developed a guilt thing and pulled away from the community.

She withdrew after that incident partially due to the guilt, partially because of the fact that the people she had hung around with were splitting and going in different directions, and because about that same time the old bar, the Carousel, closed. She then turned to being more examining within.

She knew that the incident of her sleeping with those two women and involving the guy would soon become a big part of the dirt in the community. She felt she deserved the guilt but that it was not something she had done self-consciously. It happened because of lack of knowledge. She had gone through twenty-four years of life as the Barbie-doll version of the American Dream, and those three, what they were saying was, she'd better not do that anymore. She talked regularly that spring with Gloria at the church, with Gloria doing reflective listening.

Then she met Terry who was a real closet case and she, Camille, withdrew even more into that relationship. She was also starting to work on a dissertation and that required isolation. She withdrew pretty totally and she thought she had made some changes in herself during the time since. She used to be a much more physically expressive person. For example, she'd give people hugs. But she changed that because she didn't want to give the impression of coming on to them anymore. She didn't want to get the reputation of being a playgirl. She also started feeling more settled because of her relationship with Terry. She was feeling that they were choosing to be with each other and with themselves as individuals. She was definitely not as chaotic as she had been before she left.

She had no idea of what women in the lesbian community thought of her now, or of that incident from the past, and sometimes she wondered about it. She didn't see any of the old people much. She still kept mostly to herself and with Terry. Probably what had been such a major thing in her life was a minor thing in theirs, if it came up at all. If anything, she thought maybe they just thought of her as in a fairly stable relationship with a closet case. They might think she was a little more standoffish now than she used to be. Part of it was her really being in a different place, but it was also because she felt she had been burnt, so it was partially self-protection.

From her distant observations now, she felt that to become involved in this community again would be setting herself up to be hurt, just because of all the cycles of breaking up and the cattiness. There were a few people in the community who she still had lunch with occasionally. There was a rapport there that was nice, but it was casual, the relationships were not deep. There was caring, but no deep commitment. It was only a few people, two or three. She didn't want everyone to like her now as she had before, but she did want them to feel she was nice. She wanted them to know she had changed.

There was a time back before she moved away, said Melissa, before she moved to the farm in Nebraska, when she was having a life in the community that was entirely separate from her life with the Women's Shelter and with Elinor. It was a life of being frantically social with people and verging on being an alcoholic. She felt that had to do with this being a lesbian community, because in the straight world she had never had the sort of stimulation she got from women. She had had that stimulation with individual women in the past in the sense that she had been falling in love chronically since she was fourteen, but it was only here that she had developed a sense of community and that she had felt she not only had permission to be very open and intimate with any number of people, but also that she had encouragement to do so. It seemed that the community discouraged loners.

Back before she left she was into a pattern of partying. She partied and partied and drank and played. The symptoms were obvious. She was really scared of becoming an alcoholic. She had so many different selves. She would find that one self had said one thing and another another. She was so intent on pleasing. One night at the bar she heard stories about herself that she did not like—that she was a female Casanova, someone who was totally insensitive, dangerous, who had light affairs. Some young friends of Lisa's said, "Oh, you're Melissa, this and that, and this and that." That was when it really struck her.

The sense that she was lying, being contradictory selves, came out in her relationship with Elinor. At about that time they both started seeing Kathryn. She and Elinor were thinking of moving to the country and she, Melissa, was beginning to feel some real panic about that. At about that time, too, "the family" had broken up. When Gayle and Natalie split up, she and Elinor lost what was really their community, their best couple of friends. That got to Elinor particularly and thereby to her, since she was then into feeling whatever Elinor felt.

By the time they left, there was not very much here that would have made her want to stay. That was partly because of her feeling she didn't belong to any group that was the heart of this community. She had never seemed to have a sense of struggling for anything like the others had. It was also because she couldn't walk out of the house and be anything that was clear to her. There were no politics at all at the time. The politics of the early years had completely turned into a personal routine. People's concerns seemed to be their personal relationships for the most part. (She was working at a jewelry store as a watchmaker, but work was totally unrelated. It was really convenient, too, because she could not have done anything with people, but it was easy to go to work every day and sit down and deal with little bits and pieces, then go elsewhere and be crazy.)

Looking back now, she thought that the problem was that none of them in the community had been really aware of each other's processes. For all that lack of privacy she had felt at the time before she left, she didn't think anyone was really aware of what was going on with her. Likewise, Gayle splitting up with Natalie shouldn't have been of any surprise to her best friends, but they were shocked.

That was so now too in the community, Melissa thought. People were not aware of what each other's processes were. Maybe there was something basic in them all that wanted to hide their process. Why? One reason was that one of the things they had entered the lesbian concept with was the importance of personal sharing, and they had avoided some other really crucial things. Fair fighting caught on, but it very quickly got converted. The adaptations of it in the community made it looser, less formal, less rigid, less helpful in many ways than it might have been.

So she moved away. After she left, after about a year and a half of living out on the farm with Elinor, only then could she look back on what she had actually done here. She hadn't realized before how self-destructive she had been. She hadn't realized her own pattern of sociability and self-destruction. She had just never taken any privacy, so the rejuvenation of the farm was good for her. She had had a fear of being lonely there at first, but after one and a half years she was only a little lonely.

She felt now that she would never enter a community like this again, because she was still not sure she had changed that much. She was certainly still very dependent on her surroundings. She liked what she had on the farm. She was happy doing that. She came back to town for visits once every month or six weeks—to see Kathryn, to catch up on the gossip—but she felt that this community was too incestuous and limiting. She didn't think she could have control over her life here that she needed.

She had left, said Earth. She left after a period of feeling that people didn't know how to deal with her. They were telling her everything she said was negative. During that time she got more and more introverted. She needed holding at the time. She needed reassurance that she was doing all right. She needed some indication she was appreciated. Natalie was the only person who gave that to her. Other people kept spewing forth this ideology of the community, the community—this axial of support—when she felt totally abandoned. That was when she left. She moved to Texas.

She remembered, said Gerry, being upset at the support group she had been going to because it was like everyone came there to cry out their story. She remembered at one meeting somebody asked her, "What solidified your relationship with Cynthia?" She said honesty was what did it. People continued talking. She felt, "If I'm going to bare my soul and this is what happens...." So she got up and left. That may have been the beginning of her choosing not to associate with people. She was tired of them all. Then she just didn't go anywhere.

   She withdrew and she still didn't totally understand it. She started becoming afraid to go out into groups. She started getting into fights at the bar. She was angry. She remembered going to one meeting where people were sitting around asking "What do you want this group to do?" She wasn't sure. Then she found out there was this whole individual thing she had to do. She found that she wanted to be an individual. So for a long time, quite a long time, a couple of years, she did things by herself, not with her lover Cynthia, and not with the community. She figured she just had to do that and find out what was happening with her. It was a real effort. That was how it had been for her up until very recently, even now. It was only in the last year that she'd gotten so she felt she could call someone up. But now she was going to the bar more again. It was like a second coming out.

She had felt, said Claire, that she needed to come back to the community after having been away for a year. She had to come back to see people she had run away from when she left. She felt she had to deal with the things she had run away from. It was tied to her relationships. The personal issues behind those relationships dealt with a kind of identity differentiation: separation from her family, from her previous lover, and from the woman at Marshall who had been her mentor. It was like certain personal issues were tied to certain individuals. She had to deal with those relationships in a personal way, but also with those issues.

10

Mothers and Children

She was, said Meg, more likely to give out information about being a lesbian than about being a mother. That she was gay, that she was divorced, and that she had children who did not live with her were about all the secrets she had in her whole life. The mother thing she only told people who she knew would continue to be her friends, or if it came up, if they said "What have you been doing all your life?" She also told a couple of women in the community if they were having similar troubles with their kids, like Nell.

She thought her son Dudley knew that she was a lesbian, that she always had been, said Nell. He and she had listened to a radio program once where they were talking about homosexuality. Dudley had asked her, "What is a homosexual?" She had said it was a man whose primary love went to another man, or a women whose primary love went to another woman. She was not sure he knew the word lesbian but he might. He knew the reason she and his father had split up was that she wanted to live with Judith. He knew his dad was bitter. He also knew a lot about her weaknesses, that she tended to procrastinate, for instance.

She thought that the women in the community generally had been very kind to her kids, said Helen, although Marla once told them to go away, and Lu had told half the world that she didn't like the way Helen raised them. There had always been children in the community. Bart had four kids, Elinor had a daughter. Kids straddled both inside and outside worlds, Helen felt. They were part of household, lesbian community, and outside groups. They were all three and she was too. She'd had boundary problems with them just like she had with other people. Issues arose in her relationship with them about having space for herself. She had certain kinds of concerns more because of the children, she felt, although she might have had these concerns anyway—like about people not knowing on the outside and on the job especially. She stood to lose a court battle over custody because of her lesbianism, and professionally, if her advisor at school knew, she felt he would use it adversely.

She therefore did not come out and say it. She did not use the term lesbian with her two girls, Mindy and Jane. She felt if she used the term with them and identified herself, they would use the term and that would be detrimental because children had no secrets. She had to assume that whatever she told them was going to be broadcast to the PTA. She had fears that then other mothers would not let their kids play with hers, that the effects would be very far-reaching, both for herself and for them.

Right now her oldest, Mindy, who was ten, at times displayed concern over homosexuality. Mindy was very concerned that, as she had told her, half the choir Helen directed was gay. Where the concern came from was hard to say. There was a lot of peer pressure at that age. This put pressure on Helen because she didn't particularly want Mindy to be unhappy, and she would have liked to have seen Mindy at a place where she could accept other people's life styles. She had told Mindy that people were very different, that there were many different sides of them and many different things that they did, that being gay was only one thing, that there were many others. She had told her about the danger of labeling, using as examples Jews and blacks, but Mindy didn't want to hear anymore. She thought it was boring. That was only yesterday. She had said the same things before. They just had to be said again and again.

There was one recent incident that had brought all this up. The choir was practicing at the house one Sunday about a month ago. It was very hot and some of the women had taken off their shirts. She, Helen, had taken off her shirt too. Maybe three to five women out of thirteen took their shirts off. Mindy walked in and, when she saw this, had a fit. She went into her room and would not stop screaming. Jane, Helen's youngest, kept giving her notes from Mindy in the bedroom, things like, "Put on your shirts" and "I'll not be your daughter anymore. If you love me, you'll put your shirt back on." She wouldn't stop screaming. Helen went in to her then to see what the problem was. Mindy said, "You have got to put on your shirt." At first she ignored her. She told Mindy the choir was working very hard and that she was going to keep her shirt off. She lasted about five minutes. Then she put her shirt back on and requested the others do the same.

Jane, who was eight, didn't seem to care, but Mindy thought that everyone was going to stare at her mother's breasts, Helen felt. She, Helen, thought that had to do with lesbianism, because Mindy had said at about that time, either on that occasion or another occasion, "I looked 'lesbian' up in the dictionary and all signs point to you." Mindy had told her subsequently that half the people in her choir were gay. Helen did not ask her which half.

Last year during the Arts Festival, Mindy had asked directly if she was a "lesbian," so Helen knew that Mindy knew the word, but she still didn't use it in Mindy's presence and she had asked others not to also. She felt that Mindy had a lot of problems with it right now and that labeling, when Mindy was so frightened of it, was just not necessary.

Her kids, said Francis, all boys, ages eleven, nine, and two, didn't know specifically that she was a lesbian. Her oldest son called her a women's libber. However she had made no attempt to hide her affections for other women in front of them. When she took them out to Lilith and Gayle's recently, she had talked to them about the fact that some of the women would be taking off their shirts. She had asked them how they would feel about it. They said, "Huh?" They had seen her without her shirt on.

They didn't think it was a very big deal. She had asked the women in the community not to do anything different when the boys were around than they would do when they weren't there.

As far as her children were concerned, she, Francis, had no objection to their knowing that she was a lesbian. She simply didn't want to hit them over the head by saying it. Her communication with them was good enough that she felt they would come and ask questions when they had them.

She also felt that, within the community, she would have support for any decisions she chose to make about her children: whether to leave the two older boys with their father, for instance. About a year ago when she found this community she had finally felt that here were people who could hear her saying she wanted to leave her children without being judgmental. Nonetheless she had had an initial problem with them concerning whether her children would be included in certain community events because they were boys. That occurred the weekend she decided to leave her marriage, which was over Thanksgiving this past fall. She had gotten word of the community Thanksgiving dinner from someone and she had asked Natalie if it was an open function. She told Natalie that Phil, her husband, was out of town that week and that she couldn't get a sitter and asked if she could bring the boys. Natalie had said no, because they were male children. That hadn't bothered her, Francis, at the time. Natalie had said if she wanted to call everybody who was coming and poll them, Natalie would give her the phone numbers.

She told Natalie no, that this was an issue she would deal with at some point, but not then. That was on a Monday. Then the longer she thought about it, the madder she got. She mentioned it to Gayle and Lilith at one point and they got even angrier. Then on the day of Thanksgiving, she wanted to be with the women for a while, so she went by Natalie's house after she got off work. She stayed talking with people for about half an hour and it was only as she was leaving to go home and saw Helen and her kids come in that it really hit her—that she was going home to be alone for a holiday simply because she had male children.

That day proved to be the turning point of her leaving her marriage also. She felt abandoned by the community. She called Phil, who was out of town, and asked him to come home because she was hurting. He said no, he would not do so. Then, bless their dear hearts, Lilith and Gayle came out that evening after the dinner at Natalie's and stayed for two or three hours. They talked about what had happened concerning the children. Lilith and Gayle wanted to make it a community issue. She, Francis, wanted to deal with the key individuals involved, however: Natalie first, then Gloria, and that was finally what she did. She discussed it with them from the standpoint that her biggest fear in life was emotional isolation and that she had felt totally isolated in that situation. She had felt a need for emotional support which would include her children. She thought that at that point, both Natalie and Gloria realized the difference between political ideology and political fact. They realized that if you excluded male children, at some point you excluded your sisters.

At a coffeehouse later, one of the coffeehouses that was held as a community meeting, the whole thing was discussed. Out of that, a group of the women decided to form a babysitting fund for community functions. They also decided, as a community, to include all children at some functions and they specifically talked about male children. She, Francis, wasn't at the meeting, but Nell told her about it. That was the first time she knew of that her experience on Thanksgiving became a community issue. Up until then it had been mainly a personal issue for her alone. It was primarily a painful experience that catalyzed her leaving her marriage. She had set a time frame for leaving at the start of the summer, but then when she felt abandoned by Phil and by the community, she realized that ultimately she was alone, so it really didn't matter when she left, except that she had to wait until she got a full-time job.

Also a few months later it was real interesting to her that when word went out that she was going into the hospital for surgery, it was Natalie and Jo who kept her youngest, Dennis, for ten days. It was Jo who offered to keep him, but Natalie had to consent to that, seeing as how it would be an invasion in her home as well. That was, Francis felt, a redeeming grace for Natalie.

She also felt that the entire Thanksgiving incident was unusual because normally she operated on the assumption that she was more comfortable at social events without her kids. The only times she wanted to include them were when she couldn't get a sitter, like at Thanksgiving. That feeling was similar for both straight and lesbian social occasions. She simply couldn't relax when the children were around.

She had four children, said Bart, and Pam, her lover, had four. She and Pam lived with two of Pam's four and one or more of her own, on and off. Her oldest and her daughter (her third child) knew that she was gay. She had told them. The other two knew, she was sure, but she hadn't told them. Two of Pam's children knew; the two that lived with them did not. Her relationship with Pam was naturally warm at home, but there was no touching in sight of the children. She and Pam shared the parenting to some degree. They shared a bedroom. Pam's two who lived with them were very precocious, so Bart believed they did know. They knew but they didn't; they didn't know officially. She and Pam didn't touch or kiss is front of them or tell them outright and that was for their benefit. They thought that if they were to do such things, the kids would feel uncomfortable. With the way society was, it—lesbianism—was a heavy burden to put on a child.

She thought, said Nell, that though Dudley might know the word and not have a problem with it, she still had to be very concerned about what the reaction of his peers would be. If, for example, in the future Dudley was living with Judith and herself and going to school and if he brought his buddies home, she had to be concerned about what they were going to do if he said "And this is my mother and Judith's bedroom." She hoped to hell he wouldn't end up hating her. He was a little bit angry to begin with because she gave him the name Dudley and he got teased by his peers. She was also worried that her husband would try to get Dudley away from her by saying she was an unfit mother because she was a lesbian. That was why she was taking the whole divorce thing very slowly.

She was very open with her son Chris, said Marie. He had seen the good parts of her relationships and the bad. He had his favorites of the women she dealt with. Most of them he liked. He knew the term lesbian and he knew the term gay, but you couldn't really explain that much to a seven-year-old child. It got to a point where he would walk up to people and say, "Are you gay or straight?"—mostly to her friends. She was not going to make him straight, she felt, but he had a fine appreciation for women, and he even said "women." He would catch himself when he said "girls."

Sometimes she took him to the bar. She had taken him down for Sunday brunch a few times. He'd gone upstairs and played pool with some of the women and he danced. The first time she ever took him, they were going to her mother's afterward. He understood that there were certain things they did not tell Grandma. His whole comment after they left, however, was that he really didn't understand why Grandma wouldn't like it. She told him: "Yeah, because they're good people. People are basically the same. They're labeled." Generally, she felt, he was fine about it, but there were surprises, like he came home from school one day and he said they played Screw the Queer. She said, "What?" She sat him down and they talked about it. She wanted to explain what queer meant. He said, "That's okay, but does that mean I can't play Screw the Queer anymore?" She said no.

About a year ago, recalled Vivian, she went through a traumatic siege about whether to tell her daughters. They were twenty-four and twenty-one. She wasn't comfortable with them not knowing. She had gone to visit her friend Eva in Oklahoma and when she came back, she told her daughters that her relationship with Eva was not entirely a platonic one. She didn't have to spell it out for them. The younger girl said, "Whatever turns you on." The older girl, Amy, was very upset: "Oh my God, my mother a lesbian!" Amy was not very stable herself in relationships. Since then, Amy had come around though. She was now 100 percent.

She, Vivian, had taken it gradually with Amy. She had told her at first that she was bisexual. Amy said, "Maybe that's just a phase you're going through," so Vivian went along with that, to cool her down a little. She said, "Well, you may be right," and she imagined Amy might be. She didn't think so, but she might be. Vivian knew Amy liked Eva. Eva had been up here and had spent time with her. Amy knew that Vivian was planning to move to Oklahoma to be with Eva. Amy had said to her a week or two ago, "I think you ought to tell Eva you're coming." She would make references like "I'll come to visit you and Eva."

In the beginning, however, the shock was just tremendous. Amy was basically a very liberal kind of person, Vivian felt. She would believe in homosexual rights, but when someone says "Here's your mother . . . ," that was a little different.

There was also the fact that the girls had seen their father after she told them. He'd remarried. Amy told him. She, Vivian, had told them, "Now don't say anything to anybody; this is strictly between the three of us." Then Amy told her she had told him. Vivian said, "Why did you do that?" Amy said she had to tell somebody. Later, in a letter, her father asked about a life insurance policy of which Vivian was beneficiary. He asked her to take over the premiums. She said no. He wrote another letter back after that in which he said something about "your sordid affair of last summer." It was not clearly a threat. She didn't think he wanted it out, but it was something she had to deal with.

That was one of the reasons she and Helen had this pact: that if something ever happened to either one of them, the other would go in and remove the incriminating evidence (to do with lesbianism). She, Vivian, had a key to Helen's house and Helen had a key to hers. They each felt it was best that way, given their situations.

Her mom was gay, said Lisa, and if it hadn't been for the lesbian community and the Women's Shelter, she herself would undoubtedly have been straight. The Women's Shelter was where she first began to get her strength as a person. She used to fight a lot when she was younger. She would have temper tantrums to make people do things with her. She was thirteen when the Women's Shelter started, the only one in the house that age. She was thirteen or fourteen when she realized that her mom and Melissa were having an affair. It didn't matter to her, but she didn't like Melissa. She used to fight with her mom a lot then. They would cuss and scream. She wanted attention. Her mom ignored her until she was seventeen or eighteen, but she still felt she got a lot of strength from her mom.

Mom, Melissa, Gayle, and Natalie were her family from when she was about thirteen until she was about nineteen. She got a lot of strength from the rest of them too. They were all real rational, they were happy, they had nice things. They obviously respected each other. If she hadn't had them, her mom and she might have gone on fighting and she probably would have gone straight.

Now that she was twenty and on her own, she felt that her mom, Melissa, Natalie, and Gayle, when they saw her, looked at her as just an amazement. They were used to the little girl with braces who was a real brat. They hardly believed she was an assistant manager now. She wouldn't act now like she had then. Then, for attention, or because of the hassles of being an only child, she did it. She also went with men. After that, she met Janet. When she was eighteen she brought Janet home and into the world of Mom, Melissa, and Natalie. Janet was from a different kind of background and just loved it. She had never met any gay people before and she was real happy. It was like taking a child to Disneyland. Janet would do things with her, Mom, and Melissa, constructive, creative things.

She went with Janet for a year. When they broke up she, Lisa, decided she was straight, which meant more or less leaving the world of Mom and Melissa. She felt disgusted with the relationship with Janet and she thought gay life was really hopeless, the open relationship business particularly. It had gotten to the point with Janet that they couldn't start all over because things were so bad they didn't have anything in their hearts to start with.

Her life after that was like an explosion—going to bars and getting in fights with men. She and the people she hung around with wanted to be so tough. Then she met Mike, who she was with now. Mike would come to see her at the bar. Janet matchmaked her and Mike. Janet knew Mike from high school. Mike was from the same kind of background as Janet, the rough type, the bar woman. They were different from Natalie, Jo, Melissa, and her mom, who would be classified as gay feminists. She, Lisa, still considered herself a gay feminist, though she didn't have any involvement with gay feminist people right now.

She felt that she had identified physically as a lesbian on and off through the years because in some periods she went to bed with men. Mentally, however, she had been gay since she was a kid. Right now she was strictly gay, being with Mike. She'd had a lot of crushes on women in junior high and high school. At the Women's Shelter there were a lot of gay women around and she'd had crushes on them, but the first actual relationship she had was with Janet. She had always had a lot of support for being gay, which she felt she wouldn't have had as much if her lover were a man and if she were taking him home, because her mom was gay.

When she thought about the community since her mom and Melissa had moved away, she thought about it as Natalie and Jo and all their friends. She still felt that Natalie and Jo were part of her family. There were maybe thirty of them in the larger community as she, Lisa, saw it. They were in their thirties and forties, political, radical, making pretty good money, not on welfare, middle class, rational. She didn't consider them terribly emotional people. She thought a lot of them were rationalizing more than they were getting into how they were feeling. They didn't allow themselves to feel jealously, for example, because they thought that was wrong. She had been like that for a year, but now she didn't think there was anything wrong with jealousy, anger, any of that. She hung around with a different group of people now when she wasn't working; they were younger. They were either her bar friends or the friends she had from high school.

Her bar friends came out to the trailer sometimes and she had a good time talking with them about nothing, drinking lemonade. With her old friends from high school, she talked about things that had to do with life. Neither sets were college people though. They had always thought, "Why go to college when you didn't even want to do it?"—even the ones whose parents, like hers, were middle-class liberal.

PART III

11

Bar Women and Political Women

There was, said Hollis, this whole mess of people who were known to members of the community as people who came in from outer places like the army base and got drunk. When she first moved here it was a division that was acknowledged. She was told, "These are people we see at the bars who we don't bring into our homes."

She hung around with them sometimes, said Earth. They had different values. They made a big deal about getting a new car or new clothes. They were into roles. They would see their partner or someone they were attracted to as a prize, as if they had won them. They were standoffish to her when she saw them. She felt that was because they thought she was a radical. They thought she bombed buildings because they saw her putting up posters in the bar. (She put up posters for coffeehouses in the bar sometimes.)

There were the bar people and the home group, felt Jane. She enjoyed the home group. She had met them through parties that her lover Suzanne and she had gone to. They were more a gathering of professional people than the others. She went to the bar every once in a while, but it got too rowdy and too noisy for her. She preferred the parties in the homes where people would be sitting around, playing poker, listening to music. It seemed to her that the professional people looked at life differently from the bar group. They had different goals and different ideas of how to do things.

There were definitely two groups, felt Marie. She was established in one of them, but she was interested in the other, in her radical lesbian sisters. It was not that she had chosen not to be part of that group, she had just not been exposed to it. Like during the Arts Festival—she knew there were a lot of women at the bar who didn't even know there was an Arts Festival going on. On a few of the nights of the concerts, she went down and hung around the doors of the Festival. Her friend Alison was working there as a security guard. She went in once on Saturday night and listened. It was message music. Other nights she just hung around. She was surprised to see there were that many women. She was sure there were a lot of women at the bar who didn't even know there were other gay women in town.

The women at the bar, how could she say this? Sometimes she got very disgusted with them. It could happen at a straight bar. You got the same kind of people coming to the bar. They were partiers. They were out to have a good time. She knew most of them by first name, but she didn't get too involved. She only carried on conversation like, "Hi, how's the weather?" They were friendly. They were good people. But if you wanted a discussion with them, you wouldn't have it. If you just wanted to get together and laugh and have a few drinks, they were good for that.

She was sure the feminists were like them too. The feminists could party. They were down there at the bar on Friday and Saturday nights. They were just not there as often. You didn't get to mingle with them. She got the impression that most of them were still in school. They came across as intellectuals. She liked that. She felt that was good, though she had only met a few, probably because she was the other kind. She had gone to a coffeehouse once or twice, but she was shy. She didn't know anybody, so she found it difficult. She was not the kind of person who went up and said, "Hi, I'm Marie." The few of them she knew were through her friend Alison. Alison knew both worlds. The feminists, from what she had gathered both from her own observations and from Alison, socialized more in their own little circle. A lot of it was devoted to the movement. She supposed she was apathetic in her stand as compared with them.

She felt more comfortable being with the people at the bar because that was where she had started out, which was about three and a half years ago. The woman she was seeing at the time would go down to the bar with her and they would meet people there. When that relationship went under, she had started going a lot again herself, partying a lot. In the beginning, the bar she went to was the Carousel. Then when it closed everybody migrated to Leo's. When the Orbit opened, she started going there. She worked there part-time. She liked to socialize and she really liked to dance. As it was now, she went every week; like last week she went Wednesday, Friday, Saturday, and Sunday. She went in spurts: one month she would go every night and then she would go only on a Friday or a Saturday.

Last month she was going pretty regularly every night, probably because of a woman she was interested in being there. Now that woman was going with somebody else, however (somebody she, Marie, had just broken up with), so she didn't go when she knew the two of them would be there. She had gotten the impression this last time that it was a lot of "Pass Around Patties" at the bar. Like a lot of women could go in there and have three or four women that they were intimate with be there, women they had a real intense relationship with—for a month.

That had happened with her and she'd seen it happen with other people too. One week they were with one lady, the next week it was another lady. She almost felt they were turning tricks like the guys. The last two she was with, their whole attitude was, "I don't want to get involved." They wanted to be footloose and fancy free. They both knew she was still wrapped up in her first lady, and it was like she felt they were telling her, "That's your problem." The first one had been the love of her life. They were still close. The one after her was like a nice lady. They were both still her favorite dance partners, which made it difficult too. She didn't have anyone to dance with anymore, now that the two of them (her first and second) were together. She had met both of them in the bar. She was a firm believer that you couldn't keep a relationship in the bar: if you started a relationship in the bar, it would end in the bar. Yet she continued to do it.

The bar, Marie thought, was a kind of community. They were all pretty cliquish. She thought they were probably just as cliquish in the other community too, the feminist community. She had noticed it last Friday and Saturday night when the women from the feminist community came in from the Arts Festival concerts late. They all came together, they all sat together.

At the bar, the new bar, the Orbit, the women who went upstairs were the women from the movement: the ones that wanted to be able to come to the bar and dance, drink, play pool, socialize. The women downstairs in the right-hand corner by the back door, they were more the typical bar types: they got rowdy, they were partiers. Some of them, the rowdy ones, were really into role playing. The bar people, if there was going to be a dress-up night, some of them would come in tuxes; the other ones would come in dresses. The movement women, however, would all dress similarly: very casual, not defined by roles. They would look pretty much alike. Some would be butch and some were not, but you wouldn't know for sure. With the others, the bar types, you could just about tell who was which by the way they walked across the floor and who they asked to dance, if not by dress. Butches just didn't ask another butch to dance. For herself, she liked to keep people guessing. They never knew what they were going to see her in next. Only a proportion of the bar women were like that, however, in not wanting to be typed—maybe one-quarter of them, maybe not even that.

They were definitely a different group, the bar women, thought Alison. They were different from the activists. The difference had to do with motivation. The bar women were just not motivated that other way. She knew both groups. She associated more with the bar people, but she used to go with Kelly, and Kelly was in the other group. When she was with Kelly she went to a few of their meetings and their picnics, but she just didn't have as good a time. She probably had a mental block, she thought. Something was wrong when she went. She was not really there. She found it hard to relax personally. Maybe she just hadn't grown up yet, she didn't know.

She knew mainly that she felt out of place with the activist women. She didn't think they were having enough fun. They were always doing something. They were real hyper, gung ho. A friend of hers had a name for them. Her friend called them "Right on Women." The bar people were a lot more like working class. They were down-to-earth people, though some of them had real good jobs. A lot of them she knew worked in hospitals; one was a janitor; a couple were surgery technicians; one was a secretary in a hospital. She knew radio announcers, florists, a bank balancer, a photographer, people that worked at the cheese factory and the power plant, a couple of teachers. They just seemed to her to be a happier bunch of people than the activist women.

She had a few friends from the activist group whom she did feel at ease with, however. They would sit around and have beer sometimes, or go to the movies or a play, or go swimming or walking. These ones she was familiar with were Deborah, Sam, Nikki, Stephanie, Kelly, and Judith and Nell. They weren't as bad as the others. There was also Ellen who used to be her English teacher. She knew these people were involved with the other stuff too, but when she saw them she could communicate with them. They had discussions as well as could be managed at the bar given the noise. These people, the ones she was familiar with, had time. They were different from the other activist women who were farther down the road, the ones who went to the state capitol and marched, who did everything—meetings and everything that was organized. It got done. She thought that was great. But those people were driven. She didn't know their names, except for Earth. During the day Earth might be one, but at night she was down at the bar soaking up the suds. Earth was in-between, a little like herself, Alison thought.

She, Alison, used to go the bar five nights a week. Now that she worked nights as a security guard, she only went two, not even three nights anymore. When she was going five nights, it would be weekends plus three, sometimes four, nights during the week. She played a lot of pool. She didn't go down there just to sit in the corner and see how drunk she could get. A lot of groups down there played pool; it was like a little group, their own activist group. She knew quite a few of the men. She would go at 8:00 and stay until 12:00 or 1:00. She didn't always stay until the bar closed. It depended on how much money she had and other things. She had been going regularly like this for about a year.

She would say she had been going constantly since she came out. First she went to the Carousel, then Leo's, then the Orbit. The bar was her life. She loved it. She had heard many people say that if you were a bar person, if you went to bars, it was very superficial, that there was no depth to it. She herself didn't feel that way however. She had formed 95 percent of her closest relationships in the bar. Starting out, that was where she met them. These were the people she enjoyed, the ones she had a good time with, and the bar was where she saw them. She lived in an apartment. It was uncomfortable for her simply to sit, so she went down to the bar. It was like her house. She entertained there. She loved to dance and to play pool. She didn't drink. The people she saw in the bar were an average of twenty-five years old and she had known them for two or three years, some of them since she had been here, which was four years. She had known them for a long time and she felt comfortable with them.

There were times when she had gotten fed up or when she was working and going to school that she had been just too tired to go. She had missed it then, but she had a friend, Marie, who was going fives times a week during that time. Marie would fill her in and tell her if anything really interesting had happened. She would tell her about the relationships between the people that they knew. The two of them would just carry on, talking about who was doing what, who was going where.

The bar for her, Alison felt, was different people on different nights. You never knew who was going to come in, but you would know a core group. Some of the people she saw were really into roles, but it was maybe one person out of ten. That wasn't a big thing anymore. The ones who were into it a lot, they stood out. She was not one, but she knew a few that were. She thought it was too bad, but it was the way they wanted to live. She had two friends like that and it was funny to see them. She knew them. It wasn't them; it was the way they looked. One of them was very femme and the other you couldn't pick out from a bunch of men. They had probably just fallen into it and it was comfortable for them. There were others like that too. They stood out from the activist women and from most everybody else.

The bar women generally, Alison felt, stayed in their world and didn't acknowledge the activist women when they came in. Generally they didn't think of the activist women at all; they didn't notice them in their environment. The two groups were scared of each other, she thought. They behaved very differently. The level of the women who were active was a lot higher, the mental level. They were intelligent and they used it a lot. That was perfect. That was the way it ought to be. But there were some people who didn't want to be that way all the time and those were her people, the bar group.

The people at the bar were like she was, felt Mike, many of them, especially the roughneck kids. She was a roughneck kid herself not long ago. She used to be rowdy. She drank a lot and stayed in the bar, in Leo's, most of the evening—hollering, dancing, getting into trouble, fighting. She used to get into a lot of fights: fistfights, fights over somebody hassled with her lover. She'd be real hot tempered, a lot more than she was now. She'd stand up on the table swearing, swearing and dancing.

She did it because she was new at the bar. She was meeting all these gay people for the first time and just letting go, because finally she could be in a place and be herself, because she'd found her independence after keeping it closed inside for so long.

Then things changed after she met Lisa, because Lisa was not a rowdy-type person. Lisa worked at a health food store, so she was very health conscious. She was always cramming vitamins down Mike's throat. It also changed—she, Mike, became less rowdy—because she had gotten used to it, to gay people. So it was not like she was an inventor and had just discovered them. People she met now did not as a rule know of her from her rowdy period. Now there were other people being rowdy in the bar. It was only a portion of the people who came in, but they were noticed. They liked to tear things up. Most of them had gotten thrown into being gay because of their life experiences. Like Prissy's mother was a prostitute and so Prissy started sleeping around and then got fed up with men. Sometimes they just needed attention.

There were different types who came into the bar, into Leo's, Mike felt. For two different periods she had worked there as a bartender. She was the first gay woman who worked there for a long time. She would see the different types. You had your upper-class gay people that came in, your college students, your army people, the middle-class people that lived here, the lower-class people, the dope freaks, the straight people who hadn't come out of the closet yet. Leo's had a different percent of each of these types than the Orbit. The Orbit had more of the upper-class and middle-class people who lived here. Leo's had more of the lower-class and army people, the out-of-town college students, the dope freaks.

Your more common people came to Leo's, Mike felt, and the snobs went to the Orbit. The people who wanted to look pretty went over there. The people who wanted more sex, one-night stands, they had always come to Leo's. Leo's was a more tough kind of bar but it was home to her. Most of her friends came there. She had met Lisa there. Janet, whom she knew from high school, introduced them.

Janet and Mike, Lisa felt, they both came from the same sort of background, kind of rough, close to being blue collar. Mike's friends from high school were like Mike—rough, rowdy, going out and partying every night—but Mike really came from the middle class in terms of her parents. They were alike in that, she and Mike, Lisa thought. They had a lot of friends who were in different cultures. The bar group they knew was full of tragedies, traumas. One woman she knew met a women in the bar on Wednesday and they were getting married on Sunday. They had known each other for a week. She, Lisa, used to go to the bar more during the period after she broke up with Janet, but now it was like the only reason she went was it gave her a chance to relax after work. It was like going to the laundromat to catch up on the gossip. She didn't get that involved. The main difference between the bar group and Natalie's group, she felt, was that the ones in the bar group didn't like it when their lovers screwed around, while Natalie's group, they said that was all right.

The bar women were not comfortable with the political women, felt Janet. The bar women were usually younger. They weren't into women's issues. They were lesbians sexually and in their life, but not when it came to their beliefs really. They used other words and a lot of roles sometimes. They were working class often in their outlook, even if they had good jobs, while the political women were more educated, more interested in doing something good for themselves instead of sitting around the bar drinking beer. The bar women, she felt, didn't really understand about being a woman. With them, it was like "Here I am, this is enough." The bar women got more violent. For herself, she felt inbetween the two: she understood the bar women—they were fun to party with—and she could get into being political. There were lots of bar women who didn't care about that.

The bar women and the political women, she noticed, kept their distance from each other. She saw the political women looking at the bar women in the bar sometimes and she thought they, the political women, were thinking they were better than the bar women. She liked the mixture of both groups however. She had grown up political; she came out political with Lisa, Elinor's daughter. She never went to the bar a lot at first, so she thought of herself as basically more political than she was bar, but there were things about her that were "bar-ish," liked lusting after another woman. After she split up with Lisa she had started going to the bar more. That was where she met Frankie. Frankie hung more toward the bar women. She came out that way, in a definite sexual way. Being with Frankie had made her, Janet, think a lot about the differences.

Bar women, she thought, had never even heard of the Sapphic Plains Collective or the Lavender Newsletter. Why call them "bar women"? It was their attitude. It was like finding a couple coupling. If you took lovers, you would find that the bar women, if they were wanting to do something, they were more likely to do it together, while political women were more into doing things by themselves. With bar women, if they saw a woman with another woman, it was automatically assumed that she was unfaithful; whereas political women, they just didn't wrap their self around that.

Bar women maybe had more of a tie with each other than political women, Janet felt. They were more insecure because of the way the bars were. Bar women were out to screw everybody one way or the other. They were ages seventeen to thirty. Some of the political women were eighteen and up, but there were not so many young ones; more of them were around thirty and over. Bar women were not as aware as political women. For instance, she had heard more bar women talk about dildos. In fact, she had never heard political women talk about dildos. Political women, in making love, would spend more time on you. They were more aware that it was men who were likely to pull a "Wham, bam, thank you, m'am."

She had seen the difference at parties. At bar women's parties something was always happening that didn't need to be happening. Bar women were always coupling, like, "She's my woman. Get over here." Some couple would get into an argument and the whole party would come down; or someone would do something stupid, like going and cranking up the stereo full blast when they knew the cops were going to get called; or someone would be breaking a bottle over someone else's head.

Political women's parties were more organized. Their parties could be wild too, but it was like the difference between comparing a responsible group of people and the carefree type, the type that got totally blown away, that got too rowdy. Political women dealt with things more in advance than later, Janet felt: like they'd put something away if they didn't want anything to happen to it, or like in fair fighting where everything was checked out in advance.

There was, however, a tradition with the bar women and you could follow that tradition. It was much easier than to make up new rules and roles. Like bar women had a logic that "you don't go out on your old woman." You could see it with Mike and Lisa. Mike would come up to Lisa and put her arm around her and say, "You're my woman." Political women didn't do that. Also, bar women had this way of showing affection: "Don't be touching my woman or I'm going to whip your ass," a bar woman would say. You wouldn't find political women doing that.

She, Janet, knew the political women from before when she was with Lisa. Since then, she had become more social with the bar types, mostly because she needed more support from people her own age, and because bar women were more totally let loose, they would just forget all issues.

Also, she liked to be stylish sometimes, to get all dressed up. Political women didn't care that much. Yet she still liked the education part about the political women, the spiritual part, the intellectual; she liked the way political women felt about other women. Sometimes the bar seemed to her so tight. Right now she was trying to figure out where she belonged. She hadn't found it yet. She wanted to go to more coffeehouses and political women's events and she was trying to bring Frankie along. She had taken Frankie to the Memorial Day picnic and to a party that weekend. Frankie was not the typical bar woman, Janet felt. She was more open to understanding another person's ways. Had Frankie come out in a political women atmosphere, she would have come out as a strong-minded woman, not as a role, butch, like she had with the bar women.

She and Frankie had been together now for six months. Frankie had never had a woman who had said no when she wanted to touch her before. She had never had a woman who would say she needed her own space, like when she was feeling real closed in. Bar women had put Frankie into a real macho role, Janet felt, and Frankie fell into it and let them. She didn't say, "Hey, wait a minute." Janet said to Frankie at one point, "Just go to the bar and start to think about what people are doing to you." Once when she and Frankie were there with a man/woman couple they knew, when it was time to leave, the man said, "We'll be home when we're damn good and ready," meaning he and Frankie. Afterward, Janet pointed that out to Frankie and Frankie said that she had never realized or been aware of the roles that people put her in. Frankie was used to wearing men's clothes: flannels, blue jeans, and work boots. Janet said to her, "What did those women do to you when they put you into these roles?" She had met Frankie at the bar, but they didn't get to know each other there, but at her apartment.

She had first met Janet at the bar, recalled Frankie. It was about a year and a half ago. She, Frankie, was sitting there with all her butch friends. They were encouraging her to pick someone. Janet was walking across the dance floor and she was real well put-together. She had big tits. Frankie said to the person next to her, "Look at the set of knockers on that woman." She didn't realize that was Janet at the time. It wasn't until a few times later when Janet came in with two other women they both knew that she talked to her. She and Janet were standing around. Then Janet left. When she came back, they started to talk. Most of the women in the bar liked to dance, but she, Frankie, didn't like to dance. She liked to play pool, so she asked Janet if she wanted to play pool. Janet said yes, so they played pool. They had a drink and sat and talked. Frankie was not real good with social graces, but Janet said, "You want my number?" She said yes.

It was rough in the beginning because these two other friends of theirs wanted to see Janet and someone else together, and Frankie and someone else, but it was like true love conquered all, Frankie felt. They had a wedding ceremony in the bar, she and Janet, after about a year. They gave vows to each other. They gave rings New Year's Eve at Leo's. Janet liked flairs, big productions. She kept talking to people about the wedding beforehand, telling people she and Frankie were getting married New Year's Eve in Leo's. They met in the back of the bar and each of them had someone stand up with her. It was nice, Frankie felt. Janet was real into it. She was running around the bar telling people. She wore a dress and curled her hair, even put on makeup. She, Frankie, just wore her jeans, even had patches on them, and a flannel shirt. Janet said that was all right, she loved her anyway.

Then they started living together. That was six months ago. They lived out in a trailor off I-28. Frankie was really happy with Janet. Janet was different, she thought. All the women she'd ever went with before were bar women and the only things she, Frankie, knew that had to do with gay life were the bars. She was just starting to meet this other side of lesbian life now with Janet, the political side. Janet was opening doors for her. She was interested, but she came to it different from Janet.

At first—four years ago when she was seventeen and still in high school—she had thought there was nobody. It was just her. She was the only one alive like this. Then she decided to go down and find out if there were any gay bars in town. She went to a meeting at the university and everyone went to Tiny's, a straight bar, afterward. This woman there asked her if she had ever been to the gay bar and then wrote out the name of the Carousel for her. She, Frankie, was thinking, "Oh my God, there's going to be all these women, like 6'4" Amazons." Then a group of them went to it. They sat at a table near the door. They had a really good time.

It was very opening for herself, Frankie thought. She saw that this stereotype wasn't true: that you could pick 'em out a mile away walking down the street. She saw that they weren't all truck drivers; they were like everyone else. Then about two months later, she decided that her feelings of attraction for women weren't all friendship, but she would say she was "bi." About three months after that, she was sitting and thinking and it started dawning on her. Then there was this tremendous moment of saying "Hey, you're gay," and by saying "Hey, you're gay," she knew she was bringing down on herself all those bad things people had to cope with. She was putting herself in a very "bad" position, but it was such a relief—like personally, emotionally, she wouldn't have to put up this front anymore. It was such a freedom, such a load off her shoulders.

During those months she was in the Carousel as much as she could get over there. The closer she got to feeling she was gay, the more she would go there. It got to be like every night. That was the atmosphere that she was "brought out" in. It was a real exciting time in her life. It was her introduction to gay life. These women would come up and say "You're good looking" and walk away, or they'd buy you a drink and you wouldn't expect to be with them the rest of the evening, or you'd go home with them. Bars were new to Frankie then and being in a disco and drinking were new to her. She started feeling a fellowship with these people. Even if people were mad at each other, there was still a stick-togetherness, she felt.

There was this one crowd of women that she'd hang around with. If anything happened to you, they'd put you up. It was different then from today. Back then there weren't a lot of the games there were now, like people saying they'd stab you in the back. She, Frankie, had a whole lot of friends then. She'd play pool with them. They drank together. They had a good time. When the Carousel would close for the night, a lot of times, instead of their friends going home to Queens Crossing or Painter's Creek, they'd come back to one of the houses of the people in town. They'd do things together outside the bar. It was like a mini-community. They'd get jobs for each other. She, Frankie, felt at the time like she was a giver and receiver of the best emotions women could have with each other. Like with these women, if she came up with any idea, it was listened to with a serious outlook. She had been interacting in the world for seventeen years, but this was a whole new way to interact with women.

It was sad, too, because in a way the only place they had to interact in was the bar and they'd get snockered. It was a lot of heavy drinking, but she put up with it because it was like, for once, when she said, "This is Donna, she's my friend," it meant, "If she's hungry and needs food, I'll give it to her. If she needs a place to stay, I'll put her up." It was true friendship. It ran deeply. A lot of gays, Frankie thought, had this pressure on them to stick together. Straights didn't have to develop these deep ties where you depended on each other. Like with these women, they were willing to share the burden with you, to comfort you if you needed it. Even if you were having some irrational fears, they would take you seriously. It was the first time in her life that she understood the meaning of friendship.

That period lasted until the Carousel closed, about a year's time, a little more. There were about forty women who used to go to the bar on a regular basis. People were into roles very much at the time. Almost every woman back then was into a role. She, Frankie, was used to trying to be feminine in going to straight bars, but one night she came to the Carousel in a tux and the next night she came in femme clothes. People were totally freaked out, like, "What's this kid doing to us?" She felt she was telling them she didn't want to get into those roles. She was saying, "Look, I'm Frankie." She didn't want a duplication of straight society. The first time she ever danced with a woman, she danced with Snooky and Snooky said, "Are you femme or are you butch?" She, Frankie, said, "I'm butch," because that was what she'd heard in reference to all gay women. Snooky said, "Then why aren't you leading?" It was bizarre.

After the Carousel closed, the group of them started going to Leo's. Leo's had always been the men's bar. It was small and crowded and uncomfortable, so they tried getting together at different people's houses; but then they all drifted off. She, Frankie, would just stay home a lot. She didn't really want to go to Leo's. She had this sadness in her heart, because it was gone, what they had before was gone. It was like saying good-bye to an old friend, although once in a while some of them would see each other in Leo's and the bond would still be there.

Then the Orbit opened and they started seeing each other a little more often, though the Orbit was more a big-city bar and one thing Frankie didn't like about it was straights coming in a lot. One night somebody was bothering Janet. It took everything she had to keep from picking up something and throwing it at him.

Before Janet, the bar had been her whole life, Frankie felt. She had never heard of other gay things, like the gay picnics. Then Janet came along. Janet brought her books—like *The Lesbian Reader* she bought her as a Christmas present—and records like *Lesbian Concentrate* and *The Berkeley Women's Music Collective*. She'd never heard of them before. Janet knew different people because she had come out political. She'd been exposed to ideas that Frankie had never even thought of. It shocked Janet sometimes that Frankie was totally in the dark, but Janet had a lot of fun teaching her things. Janet would bring home stuff for her to read, or sometimes they'd just sit by themselves and get into this talk about women. It was really eye-opening, Frankie thought.

She thought the reason Janet and she were real close and their relationship was working out so well was because they talked. They could communicate. They were willing to listen to each other's ideas—like when Janet would start talking political stuff, she, Frankie, would listen and try to understand. A lot of people wouldn't want to put out the energy to try to understand.

And what was especially nice about it was that she, Frankie, was not stumbling haphazardly through it by herself; somebody was there to give her guidelines. Though she knew if she really wanted to get into it by herself, Janet would feel, "It's all right. Go ahead and grow."

The bar, Frankie felt, was a thing that if you wanted to do something on a regular basis, it was always there. Now, however, she was getting interested in "When is there going to be another picnic?" or "Let's do something by ourselves." She was realizing that you didn't have to drink just because you were gay. Last year she went to one of the Arts Festival concerts and she felt a kind of closeness for womankind. She had liked that a lot.

She was, she thought, an idealist. She believed in true love. She was always looking for the field without the thorns. She believed in pure things, like loyalty. If someone was a true friend, it really moved her. She was a dreamer. She was always searching for that true white love. Janet was real practical, but she, Frankie, thought there were more important things than practicality; like feelings for her were very real, more real than "reality." Janet was having dreams now about starting a business. Frankie read her Aristotle and Plato. She felt she could apply that kind of stuff to life; whereas to Janet, it wasn't very useful. Janet and her, they were very complementary, Frankie thought. Janet was the practical one, she was the dreamer, and all of it was like puzzle pieces. It was real tight. You fit.

12

The Outside World, I

WORK

She usually kept it to herself, said Jane. She wanted to avoid trouble. When she had worked as a nurse, she had kept it to herself. Now she and Suzanne ran a crafts shop on the edge of town. They got caught once in the shop. This customer went out to her car for something and when she came back, the two of them were kissing. They all handled it very well however. They acted like nothing had happened.

It was a small town, said Terry. That was one reason she didn't go to the bar. Helen had told her, "Well, if anyone sees you there, they're there for a reason too," but she, Terry, felt she had to be conservative. She was in a highly conservative field, higher education administration. Education generally was conservative. She had to worry about her career. She expected that a lot of people in her department, especially the ones who were also in the closet, who would be the toughest, they'd jump all over her. She'd also have to deal with the men. For them, there was something discomforting about a woman who didn't need a man. An additional concern she had was that she was responsible for 900 undergraduate students, most of whom were dealing with their own sexuality, and their parents might be upset.

In terms of her job, said Cynthia, she felt her boss would be patted on the back if it were known that she, Cynthia, had a criminal record, because their agency was for criminal justice.

But let one of them know that she was gay and that would be that. "Ex-con" had considerably less stigma as a label than being gay. She knew this because she had gotten jobs because she was an ex-con and lost them because she was gay.

She did not, said Lucy, want to be dealt with as Lucy Lesbian on her job. She wanted to be dealt with as Lucy Artist-Editor-Printer. She had enough to deal with on her job as it was. She was not really afraid of losing her job. She thought they had all been aware for a long time, the ones with the power to hire and fire. It was a matter of her not wanting to deal with their responses.

She had tenure, said Diana. She wasn't worried about that, but about the reaction she expected from these superconservative students where she taught. They were religious; they were bigots—not all of them, but a few examples. They could make teaching hard. It was tense enough for her as it was. A lot of the students came in hostile toward grammar to begin with and hostile toward her because she was teaching. She didn't need anything more.

At work they didn't know, said Ginger, although she thought they might think she was. Her boss might know. It was possible for him to figure out that she and Leah spent a lot of time together. The company, the printing company where she worked, was fairly liberal; there were gay stockholders. Joan Harvey, who was one of the best printers in this town, was gay. She worked for another company, but her boss knew Joan. In addition, Betty, the woman Ginger's boss was living with, was the captain of the softball team Ginger was on, so Ginger felt he might know through her. She herself hadn't told him, however, because she felt that her social life, which encompassed her sexual life, was none of his damn business. She wanted to be friendly with him, but she did think there was a limit. She would probably never invite him over to dinner, or any of his three sons who worked in the shop. The fact that she had been involved with Betty's softball team meant her social life was seeable outside the work atmosphere, but that was the closest her employer would ever come, because that was the way she wanted it.

She worked at Ohlone's, the cheese factory, said Leah. Jenny worked there too, but nobody at Ohlone's knew. It was real important to her that nobody there knew, because she didn't have any union and it was the only job she had and she didn't want to lose it. There were a lot of women out there and they talked about their boyfriends. She would talk about the Arts Festival; she would talk about women. Lately, though, she'd also talk about men, to balance it out, so they'd get the idea she did know a couple. Last week Jenny buzzed over and they talked about the Memorial Day picnic. Jenny asked her when she was going to have dinner (they both worked the night shift) and, for the first time in her life, she had a sisterly feeling. It was beautiful. There was another woman working out there who was gay too—Lurline—but she avoided Jenny and herself.

Nobody knew at Ohlone's, Leah felt, but she'd recently sensed that maybe some of the women she worked with suspected. She was laid off for two months, and when she came back, these women seemed more interested in her or something. She thought maybe they had talked about it while she was gone because, before she was laid off, Ginger, her lover, was living on the west side of town and she was living on the east side and she had needed a way to get back to Ginger's house every night. People at work knew she lived on the east side. Because of that, to cover herself, she had told them that it was hard to get to the east side at that time of night and that she needed a ride to a friend's house on the west side who let her camp out there.

This one woman she worked with, Mimi, would take her to Ginger's. Sometimes two of the women would come along. They would give her a ride and drop her off. It didn't occur to her, Leah, at the time, but it did after she came back, that it might have seemed real fishy to them. Sometimes she would tell them when they dropped her off that there was a group of people she partied with who lived at Ginger's. One time, however, she forgot her key and she had to go back to Mimi's house to call Ginger. Mimi then knew there was only one person who lived at that house. Maybe that was why when she, Leah, came back after she was laid off, she had felt that Mimi and the other women at work were noticing and watching her more. It could have been she was just noticing them more, but she had this funny feeling.

The other night, recalled Jenny, Leah—you know Leah who also worked at Ohlone's—Leah was looking at her from across the room. It was like they were in a secret society. There were a few gay people out at Ohlone's, but mostly they were straights. If things got too close, you just shut up, even with the gay people. Being gay you led a double life, Jenny felt, or she did, which meant playing along. Her boss, he had only one thing on his mind—sex and women. She played along with the jokes. It was hard.

At first when she started working at the hospital as a maid, said Edwina, she had been very quiet with the other maids. She would listen to them talking about men. Then gradually she began to talk to some of the ladies. She started saying, "You know, I'm gay." It took her a while to get used to it. Her manager still didn't know, but people talked, so she thought he might find out. The only consequence she expected from it was that he would ask her and she would say "That's right." There had been two housekeepers out there caught kissing once. Her manager had said, "We're going to have to talk to them about that. After 4:00 P.M. it's their business, but they can't do that here," so she felt he was a righteous person.

She was a nurse at the same hospital as Edwina, said Vivian. People there didn't know about her, except for Edwina. There was also another woman at the hospital who, like Edwina, was open to people. She, Vivian, and this woman had a relationship once which was real brief. They didn't have anything in common. They were still good friends though. People saw her talking with this woman, but she thought they didn't know about her because of the fact that she had been married and had a couple of kids. That was probably the best cover she could ever have, and also her age, that she was fifty-one.

She was an operating room technician, said Marie. People at work sat around talking about their boyfriends and she talked about the girls. She played with them, joked with them. A lot of the people knew her from before. She had been at the same hospital for ten years. They had seen her come out of high school, get married, have a baby. She thought it had given them a whole new outlook on homosexuals.

She didn't tell people at her jobs that she was a lesbian, said Mitzi. She tried to say everything but that. Sometimes she wanted to talk about it with the women, though, so she used other words. She just never said she was a lesbian or used the label because she was worried she would lose her job—cleaning houses. People would be scared for her to come into the house. If they knew and she didn't say it, however, it didn't put her in jeopardy. It was just too scary to hear, she felt. If you said you were a lesbian, people got worried about the word and forgot what you were telling them. It, the word, blocked out their perceptions and distorted them.

She knew this from previous experience. She had not hired gay people herself when she had worked as a manager of Burger Town (for seven years) and Burger Heaven (for three years). She had turned down a gay man at Burger Town. She expected he would not work out and she didn't want to go through it—all the extra time and energy it would take to deal with the peer pressure against it. That was before she was acknowledging that she was a lesbian. Then at Burger Heaven there was a woman who wanted an assistant manager position who she had turned down. Part of why she did it was that she was worried about putting her own job in jeopardy by hiring a woman whom she thought people would recognize as a lesbian; this woman had a bull dyke image. And she herself was a lesbian at the time.

She wouldn't do that kind of thing now, felt Mitzi, but that was why she didn't work at real jobs anymore. In those positions she couldn't say how she felt. She had to live up to a role if she was going to be a manager, and she felt that people wouldn't hire her at all if she said she was a lesbian from day one.

She worked in early childhood, said Roxanne. It was very difficult to survive in early childhood as a lesbian, so she didn't wear Levi's to school; she wore pantsuits. Also, she wore makeup. One of her good friends was a Catholic nun, which wouldn't make people think she was gay. Most people perceived her as very religious, she felt, because this woman was a good friend.

People knew at the elementary school where she worked, said Marla, because they were pretty liberal, but they didn't know in her department at the university, where they were mostly men. They might suspect, however, because when she went to events and they said bring a friend, she would bring a woman. When she went to the first cocktail party at the start of the year, she had brought Ellen; when she went to the picnic at the end, she would probably bring Emily.

Nonetheless it bothered her that she couldn't be more open and just tell everyone. She felt that other people shared their lives and made friends and spent comfortable social times and that she was this big enigma and she just had to stay that way. It had a lot to do with the fact that most other people at the university seemed to her real straight. She was not averse to telling them if it seemed they would hear her and feel it was okay. She was averse if it seemed like they were going to jeopardize her, like in passing exams or in recommendations for jobs. As a Ph.D. candidate, she had to do a lot of things that could be judged arbitrarily.

She had come out in two of her classes, but these were classes in departments other than her own. In a library science class, she had said she was a lesbian and talked about lesbians in high school. People were very cool to her both after and before, but the teacher was real sweet. The teacher kind of pushed her into it. She, Marla, had brought in some books and had them sitting on her desk and the teacher said, "Marla, are you going to share those books with us?" Then when the teacher told the class, she said, "Marla has something she wants to tell us."

In another class they were reading this case about an old woman who was a spinster and she, Marla, had objected to the fact that it implied this woman was a lesbian and that she was judged negatively for it. In that case, when she objected, the fact that she, Marla, was a lesbian was implied, even though she didn't say so explicitly to the class. Sometimes she felt more comfortable when she didn't say it explicitly, but when they did know. Then she could have some kind of support with people. She needed to share with people, Marla felt. Being a lesbian and a feminist was an enormous part of her life. If she didn't share it, she felt like she was a different person.

When she was first going with Shelah, recalled Carol, she'd had to be more closety around her department at the university than she might have been if it were just herself. She would have felt more comfortable about taking the chance if she were alone, but Shelah wouldn't have. Shelah was in the same department and Shelah had a history of not being up front about it, though Shelah assumed that everybody knew. That was what bothered her, Carol, about the whole thing. She felt it was stupid. You got the worst of everything. You had some of the paranoia because there was doubt; there was always this question "Do they or don't they know?" While if people were to know, then they could do things that included you socially and they wouldn't do things inadvertently that would upset you.

If you were up front about it, Carol felt, you were saying it was okay, but by not acknowledging it, it was like implying it was not okay, like having a prison record. It was the worry that was the problem. Operating on the basis of having to hide, you always had to worry.

Generally, said Gayle, she didn't tell a person until she trusted them and she made a decision on trust fairly quickly. Her whole board of directors at the Women's Shelter knew, but increasingly they had to be very careful because the Shelter had this image. "Lesbian Hotel" was what people called them. Several years ago, they had been very open at the Shelter, but their funding sources had subsequently put pressure on them by innuendo. They found that every funding source they went to, every speaking engagement they went to, every agency they went to, would sooner or later bring up the issue. "Is it true you have lesbians over there?" or "I'm not sure we should send so-and-so over there. I'm not sure she wouldn't get seduced." She would tell them that in every women's organization you got involved with, you always heard that issue. Then she'd come back and cry about it. She spent a lot of time worrying about whether you should tell the Nazis you were a Jew.

She was not out at her church, said Gloria. She was out only to about four people: the woman who did ministry for women there and three women in a weekly theology group. Other than that, she was not out at the church. She had been married when she first came here and she felt that the bulk of the people in the church who saw her on Sunday mornings probably still thought she was married. When she stopped being married and became gay, she had not announced it. She had not told them. It would have been very awkward. How would you say, "This woman who has been speaking to you every Sunday . . ."? She had told the staff and the people who needed to know, but somehow she wanted to leave this job without the hassle of having announced that she was a lesbian. She had taught courses on homosexuality and Christianity, she had counseled gay people, and the coffeehouse was in the church, so she was associated with the gay community. She thought anyone who knew her, who saw the people who came in and out of her office and knew that she was separated from Ken, would put it together, but nobody had come in and asked.

The political situation in the church was such that if she announced publicly that she was a lesbian, she would probably lose her ordination. If she whispered it to the bishop, it might be all right, but he would be very careful about where he placed her and he'd say not to tell anyone. If she just talked about being woman-identified and never said the word lesbian in relation to herself, she could be tolerated on the fringe of the church.

What she wanted to do this summer when she and Leslie went away was to decide whether she wanted to be on the fringe of the church or not. She was feeling now that she wanted to be out and if she could stay on the fringe of the church and have it be all right, that was okay. She would love to do ministry with lesbians or ministry with women, as a lesbian, and be paid for it, but it remained to be seen whether that would be possible. If she came out in the church, she would have to tell her parents. Her father was also a minister.

No one at work, she believed, knew that she was gay, said Pat. She had been with the police department for nearly two years. She definitely led a double life. She had to change gears a lot during the day. She thought it would be extremely difficult for her to live with work if anybody there were to know. She didn't think she would be fired. She thought the furor would subside after a while, but work was real strange. She didn't think they suspected. She had a couple of male friends that she hung around with. People at work had seen her with them, so it was easy for them to get the idea that she was straight. They did see her with women but not in such a way that they would pick it up. She was not extremely publicly affectionate with anyone.

She had been really affected recently, though, when one of the officers she worked with committed suicide. He left a letter stating that he committed suicide because he was bisexual. He was very popular, a good police officer, not abusive, very fair with people. She would have thought that would have shocked the rest of them into their senses, but it didn't. She was going around ranting and raving for a while: "If you didn't all make fun of fags and queers all the time, maybe he could have talked to you." She didn't think she endangered her situation by saying that however. She just sounded like she liked the guy.

At work, said Natalie, she did not share. She did not hang around there. She thought that people in her department at

Marshall had probably gotten the message that her main life was elsewhere. She did not say she was a lesbian, but she thought that people had probably gotten the impression she was, because she was one of two or three visible feminists behind everything that happened at Marshall. She did not tell people because of concerns about her job and also because she had a sense of mission when talking about these things—that she'd rather identify herself as a radical feminist than a lesbian feminist and, increasingly, she didn't want to put out the energy to deal with the response, the bigotry. She wanted people to deal with her without having some prejudiced reaction intervening. She was not trusting of the outside world very much and of people's perceptions of lesbianism in particular. This distrust came from her experience of having dealt with it in the past.

If someone were to come up and ask her at work, she would tell them so far as saying yes, but she wouldn't volunteer the information or say directly "I am a lesbian." She admired people who came out and did that. For herself, however, although she openly lived as a lesbian, she didn't proclaim it. She didn't trust what people would do with the term. If they got to know her and discovered it, that would be all right, but she still feared use of the term.

People had known that she was a lesbian, said Ellen, since she got kicked out of college fifteen years ago for having a relationship with another woman student. That was a little college in the southern part of the state. She transferred to a different school after that and was paranoid about being found out. Then when she came here to teach at Marshall eight years ago, while she was not really out, she was a lot less careful and a lot less worried about people knowing than she had been before. This was partly because the woman she was with at the time was more or less out in her department at the university.

Things didn't change a great deal until about four years ago when she, Ellen, started being more out at the Modern Language Association National Convention with the Gay Caucus; she started speaking about the need for teaching lesbian literature.

151

One of the reasons she did it was for release: to try to get rid of the paranoia she still had. If you were out of the closet yourself, she felt, you couldn't be paranoid about other people forcing you out. There were also educational reasons: so other people would know; and she had an urge to be recognized as a lesbian person, as who she was, she supposed.

Being out was invigorating, but it also took a lot of energy, she found. In every spurt of talking to people—for a lesbian literature class, every little thing she did—she worried about defending herself, because she was real vulnerable as a lesbian, no matter how out she was. She was especially vulnerable to attack by students. In a course evaluation this last semester, nine out of twenty-seven students in a women's literature class she taught expressed disapproval or discomfort ranging from mild to severe over too much lesbian or feminist course content. There had been three days of *Rubyfruit Jungle* and two days of Adrienne Rich (feminist poems only), a total of five days in the course. That was the risk. It was not whether somebody would go to her boss and she would be fired. It was the risk of disapproval and rejection of her, of herself as a person. In this class, she hadn't come out. She had come out to two or three people individually, but not to the class as a whole. She had not come out in the class, but it was still a risk because if they rejected the lesbian literature, it was not only the literature, it was an attack on her. She was vulnerable to that.

In addition, she was even more vulnerable in professional groups. That was less so if she was asked in advance to talk specifically about lesbianism. Where it was hardest, in both professional situations and in classes, was where it was borderline: when she was not out to begin with and she had to introduce some subject matter that was lesbian on her own initiative. That was the hardest, but in the future she would continue to do it.

She did worry about losing her job. She worried even though she had tenure, but that wasn't the real problem in terms of employment. The real problem was getting another job—what to do with all that involvement in gay things if she had to look again.

When she had started applying for jobs after finishing school, recalled Millicent, she began thinking about whether she should or should not put her gay organizational activities (the Gay Phoneline specifically) on her resume. She talked to people and they said "Don't do it," but she chose to do it anyway. She did get a job, as a case worker in criminal justice. That was one year ago. The gay activities weren't on her resume now, however, because the jobs she was applying for now were more political, more conservative, right wing and straight, like working for the county health center. She was very aware now of being in a town where the supply of social workers was greater than the demand. She was also aware of having come through a change.

Three years ago while she, Millicent, was at the university, she was very public as a lesbian. She organized the Gay Phoneline and spoke to groups. The impetus for it was that she felt the more people who said they were gay, the more the world would be turned around, and she had felt it was her part to say it. She felt that young people who were coming out needed to see others who were gay so they could feel better about themselves. That was what she was saying then, not the political thing. She felt what those younger people needed was to see people who were comfortable about being gay and that was what she was: she was comfortable about it.

At the same time she thought that this community—the broader area—was more liberal than it actually was. There were good things that happened to her as a result of being a public gay person. She had met Cheryl, her present lover, once when she was speaking at the health center. A lot of people had come up after times she had spoken and said they appreciated what she was doing. At the beginning they would say, "This must be hard for you," and she would say it wasn't, but at the end it was. It became harder and harder as time went on, because the more she spoke, the more she saw that people did indeed have negative reactions to gay people. Prior to that she guessed she had kept herself in a very protected position, but she soon began to be more sensitive to where people were coming from when they asked questions. As she got to know more and more people through her public contacts, she got to know more about people and she stopped taking them on the surface. She found out that people who said they were understanding were not necessarily so.

That was why, said Chip, she simply did not trust them. She would not, at work, say she was a lesbian and proud of it. She worked for the state employment service. By the same token, she would not stand still and hear homosexual jokes. She would say, "That's full of shit." People knew she would not stand for that. She would have done this whether she was a lesbian or not. Why not say she was a lesbian? She supposed it was a rationalization (because she thought she should say it; she thought everyone who was gay should), but she just didn't think people should know about her sex life. It was none of their business, and she just didn't trust them. She didn't trust people—the society—not to use that information against her. Why? What did she expect would happen? She was not afraid of losing her job. The fear was of being exposed, of leaving open a part of her that was none of their business, a part that was really personal, really private.

She did not, said Nikki, think that fear of telling people you were gay ought to be overcome, because it was not the topic of homosexuality per se that mattered. It was the fear of having something too personal exposed. That fear did not affect her at work right now, because her work was washing dishes at the gay bar, but at other times it had.

Where she worked as a receptionist, said Shelah, she had never announced it. She didn't know if people knew. She thought they knew if they wanted to. She didn't think it bothered her a whole lot one way or the other, although sometimes she thought that was a really unrealistic attitude; she'd pay for it.

13

The Outside World, II

FAMILIES, FRIENDS, AND
STRAIGHT SOCIETY

Her family didn't know, said Lilith, which meant she had not told them. She had perceived that they just didn't want to be confronted with it.

Her family knew, felt Cheryl; she was sure they did, but they would probably not ask or say anything about it in any way that would make either of them uncomfortable, and she probably would never come out to them. She didn't think doing so would benefit her relationship with them. The relationship would go fine the way it was. If she came out to them in words, the whole tone of the relationship would change, because then it (her lesbianism) would be official.

She had said something to her sister and her brother, but not to her parents, recalled Norah. She thought her parents, if she told them, might be upset and worry. They would wonder, "Why did she turn out like this?" Also, she didn't really feel the need to tell them. She had felt that need for a long time at first, but it had gone away.

She had gone from her family knowing—from being totally out of the closet with them—to telling them she was not with anyone, said Camille. Because of that, they thought she had just gone through a phase.

Her mother did ask her two and a half years ago, recalled Chip. She told her mother at that time that she didn't know, because her mother had told her once before how she felt about lesbians: that they were either sick or living in sin. More recently, though, she had asked her mother how her mother would feel if she told her she was one, to which her mother had replied, "Well, you are still my daughter." That had been enough for her.

Her family knew, said Connie. They found out. They got hold of one of her letters once. It happened to be the most explicit letter she had ever received. She was living at home in a small town near Queens Crossing and working and going to school. Somehow her parents thought she would straighten up. Then when she moved here to take a job, they thought it was all over. Little did they know she was moving to a bigger lesbian community.

Her dad, said Natalie, he thought she was a spinster divorced woman living with another woman. Her mother knew and was living with it and had accepted it. She had told her mother "I am a lesbian" right out four years ago.

Her family didn't know it to talk about it, felt Martha, but they had had a number of hints over the years, including lesbian posters on her walls and how she talked about certain women. She hadn't said it, but she thought her mother knew, was not comfortable with it and didn't want to talk about it, but knew. She had been most open about it when she lived in the Free Woman's House. She had thought about telling her parents then, but by the time all that was over, it just didn't seem all that necessary; also she didn't feel especially close to her parents. In general, she felt that they knew and they were not saying anything about it, and that indicated they didn't want to talk about it. They also seemed elderly to her in a lot of ways and withdrawn from the world, and she worried that her father would have a heart attack if she were to tell them.

Her parents didn't know that she was a lesbian, but they knew she was a feminist, said Marla. They might know she was a lesbian, but they didn't or they would have been really upset. They had all the information they needed, but they just didn't put two and two together. Fear of their becoming physically ill stopped her from telling them. A projection of that would be fear of them dying and her spending the rest of her life feeling guilty. Her parents got sick a lot when they were upset. They were in their mid-sixties. In the past when she had done things that had upset them they had gotten physically ill, so she didn't see why they needed to know. It would only give them a pain.

She had given this interview about gay politics to the university paper back when she was active in the campus gay organization, recalled Millicent. It was picked up in the big-city papers. She got a phone call at 3:00 A.M. one morning from one of the papers. The first thing they asked was "Is this Millicent Johnson?" She said, "Yes." Then it occurred to her that her father might read the story. He was sick and her mother had asked that she not tell him because he would get upset and have a heart attack or a stroke and die, so she was worried. But that was not the real reason. The real reason was that she was scared of her father. If he found out, it would be very uncomfortable, but that was a whole other issue.

She had told her sister right off, recalled Jimi, and she'd been trying strategic means of telling her parents since then. She was "strategic" because she thought it would blow them away to know and she didn't want to be blown away while they were being blown away. She was just telling them what she could tell them and waiting for them to ask her.

Her mom knew, said Mitzi. She had told her last spring. She told her because she had always shared things with her mom and she thought this was a really huge change in her life and her mom should know. It had, however, taken her two years to build up the confidence to do it.

Her family knew, said Edwina. There had been some problem, but she had wanted not to be asked "Where's your boyfriend?" each time she came home. She also thought that when she told her mother she was being real radical, to hurt her. She thought her mother was still wondering if she was going to be like this for the rest of her life or if it was just a stage.

She had shared that information with her family about two years ago, recalled Lillian. She was heavy into her relationship with Opal at the time and it seemed like that relationship would be a very together, forever thing and she thought if something ever happened to Opal or herself and Opal needed her family as a support system, that wouldn't be the time to break the news to them. For example, if she was involved in an accident and there was a funeral, she wouldn't want Opal to have to sit in the back with nobody knowing.

She had to be careful about her family knowing who her friends were, said Stacy. Though she wasn't a lesbian, her closest friends were. With her family, she might be talking about a friend, she might say, "Natalie and Jo live here," or mention a female couple. She never used any word that would upset them, however, and they never asked. In a way she felt she was safe because she was married, but then in the back of her mind there was always some worry that they might think, "Here's our model daughter, hanging around with all these lesbians."

She had come out all the way as far as she was concerned, felt Ruth. She had done a lot of public speaking. She had gone on television—"Hi, I'm a lesbian, isn't that great?"—because of this feeling she had that it was important to have role models that were absent when she was in high school. But the hardest thing for her had been her parents. She had just talked to her mother about it for the first time two weeks ago, because it got to the point where she'd be going on TV and just minutes before, she'd be feeling, "Is this going to play in Plainsville? Sorry, I can't do it."

Her family, felt Chandra, didn't know; at least it had not been talked about, but her feeling was her mother would have some knowledge. In her family it had always been assumed, but the label had not been used and she was not going to change that. There were elements of risk in telling them outright that she didn't want to tamper with. She didn't think she would be fired by the family, but she also didn't want to spend hours and hours in great debate and struggling and putting her mother through lots of guilt.

She hadn't told her mother, but she thought her mother knew, said Diana. Her brother knew. At work her ex-boss knew. His wife had tried to have an affair with her. He had found out and had then tried to get her, Diana, kicked out. It had taken her a long time, however, to let people in general know, to tell friends, straight friends. She had first told her friends about two to three years ago and their response was "I know; it's about time you started talking about it." She had just been real cautious. In many ways, she still was.

There were probably friends of hers who still didn't know, felt Jimi, but anybody who was an important friend found out. She didn't tell people about it long-distance however. She only did it when they were face-to-face and could talk.

She had recently told a friend, said Aurora, and it confirmed all her fears. Once before, too, she had lost a good friend.

With straight friends, felt Meg, if she saw them as somebody she wanted to continue to be friends with, she told them, because she wanted them to know her. It was part of the friendship. Otherwise, she didn't.

It wasn't the same as at work, felt Jessica, but telling straight friends or people in general was still hard. She didn't directly tell anyone. She didn't trust their responses. It was such a big deal to tell people that kind of thing. It was uncomfortable. It was so dramatic. You didn't know how they were going to take it. If they got close enough, they would know; but she wouldn't come out and say it.

She had rarely had friends who didn't eventually know she was gay, said Deborah.

She didn't mind if people knew, said Kelly. She just didn't want to have to tell them.

When she was in high school most of her friends, when they heard she was gay, dropped out, recalled Mike. They called her a lezzie. It hurt her a lot.

People by association, felt Irene, thought she was a dyke. She had been on TV when Bronwyn and Valerie were put in jail for not divulging a raped person's name. She was with members of the lesbian community who were picketing the jail. She had also picketed City Hall about the gay rights ordinance. People had seen her who were straight. One of them asked her right out, "Are you a lesbian?" The question was really offensive to her. She asked him what he meant by it and then she just refused to say whether she was or not.

She was cautious, said Leslie. She was starting to get political, like she had been on television once, but she preferred to do it on a one-to-one basis. She was not a screaming dyke. She didn't wear dyke buttons. She thought that the outside world, the only thing they cared about was your sexuality. She might as well wear a button saying she masturbated five times a day.

Everybody concentrated on the difference, felt Jane, and they forgot that in living their lives day to day, lesbians and straight people were pretty much the same. Gay people had the same problems of why their relationships worked and of making a living that everyone else had. What was wrong was when people tended to focus on gay people because of their sexual preference and when they made that the central thing and judged it.

The outside world, felt Stephanie, even if they knew, would never really understand what went on in a lesbian community. They were constantly perceiving the community as odd, so they were constantly looking through a tinted glass. The lesbian community was a subculture and they were that way for a reason: because at this point in time lesbians as a group were threatened.

She had learned about that early, thought Earth. She'd had a job as a handywoman at a Girl Scout camp when she was younger and she took two women to a bar one night. They told the camp director and she got fired for being a lesbian. That really frightened her because that was the first time she had been out of the university connection. They removed her bodily from her tent. They pulled her car up to the tent and wouldn't let her go anywhere but the back seat of the car. Meanwhile she was yelling. She threw her tools across the tent. She was ferocious. After that, she came back to town. The Free Woman's House had started and they took her in and nurtured her for a while.

It was disillusioning, felt Jill. She would walk down the street holding hands with a friend and someone would say "fag" or "queer." At first she'd thought if it could happen anywhere, it would be in a college town. Then she thought of where these people came from—farm communities and conservative homes. She didn't think it was flaunting. She felt like when she was walking down the street holding hands, someone else might think, "Why don't I?" They had to push each other that way; they had to give each other little kicks.

Six years ago when someone would hug her on the street, recalled Ruby, she had felt petrified. There was no lesbian community here then. Later, through the Women's Shelter with more people coming out, it was like courage, models—other people did it too—and a lot of the women were younger. They hadn't grown up with the same horror stories she had.

She had noticed a difference in the past year, felt Meg. It used to be when she would walk across the campus, she would feel people felt disgust, like a real distaste, if they picked up that she was a lesbian. Now she felt they would have positive feelings. They might admire her for her bravery. She saw women looking at her now who she was sure were straight, younger women, and she felt they were flirting with her—looking in her eyes and flirting with her. She didn't know if they had changed or if she had changed. It was partly psychological. It was a cool thing. She was able to look women in the face now and get positive responses. Maybe she was just flirting, but she had noticed there was a change. She didn't know if the world was changing or if it was her. All she knew was that she felt better.

From what people said, it seemed to be a battle against the outside world, said June. At the same time, she had these fantasies of everyone being turned on and accepting and it would be okay, like on a big holiday. Her vision was of the lesbian community getting bigger and bigger and being part of the outside world, instead of apart from it. Her involvement with the community had made her realize, however, that change came in small increments. It also had brought her to understand a separatist point of view—like wanting a private society and getting strength together and celebrating your differences. Nonetheless, she felt that you couldn't live apart from this society totally, so in a way she was glad this community existed in an urban-type area with a lot of people around. It was good for exposure, the outside world's exposure to lesbians.

The outside world invaded, felt Allison. Straight people, they came to the bar. They'd hang around for a while and then they'd run for the door, or they'd make loud comments and laugh and snicker. Like she'd heard a woman say, "I'm not going in that bathroom alone." She wouldn't grab a woman like that. They thought they were irresistible, straight people. They would tend to come in groups. Wednesday was a big night because it was half-price night. It brought them out. She had seen some women in the bar once who she knew from Marshall, who she knew were straight. She made it a point to go up to them and say hello and welcome and they didn't say anything. None of them stood there and talked with her, and they'd sat across from each other for six or eight months at school. It had really bothered her, like she felt this was a gay bar and it should be for gay people, with the few exceptions being people who were just so wonderful it didn't matter who they were. If straight people came in, if they wanted to look around, she would want it if they came with an open mind and not just to see what went on.

Her awareness of it had been gradual, thought Lorraine, her awareness of what it meant to be gay. She had started from almost a zero point, from almost no awareness and certainly no correct perceptions. It was a long time before she came to understand that it was more than sexuality, that it was a life style and an emotional orientation—a whole new realm of possibility. Her first reaction when she had started meeting all these gay women had been "If that's their bag man. . . ." She didn't have any understanding. She didn't have any awareness of her own gay feelings. She simply liked the women. She liked that they liked her, that they took her seriously, that they valued her ideas, her talents.

People would not tend to realize, felt Sam, that you didn't just walk in the door, that you had to go through this long process, this transition from the heterosexual world to the lesbian world. In her case it had been harsh, like being stripped down to the core of her being. She was constantly having to confront things she hadn't wanted to see about herself before, but she was ready for it. She felt that she needed to recognize these things. She needed to leave the farmhouse where she had been living with Mary Jean and move into town by herself. She started meeting people in the community then. She hadn't had any reference for gay relationships before.

She was real aware, said Marla, of wanting to protect the privacy of the community from the outside world.

14

Privacy

Privacy, said Shelah, was having control over an amount of space metaphorically, and a lot of times physically as well. It was a space you could have control over by deciding whether to let people in and out. The mental picture she had was of one person sitting in one room in quiet. It didn't have to be a physical room; it could be a mental room. Thought played a big part in it. This person was alone and free to think in silence. It was an interplay between this space around you, which might or might not be part of you, and you.

It was, felt Claire, a sense of individual freedom and a respect for one's individuality and one's personhood. In a positive sense privacy was freedom to be yourself and, in a negative sense, freedom from prescription and intrusion by others. It was a respect for the individual's whole self. She had thought of it at first as the notion of solitude and having the right to expect someone to knock at the door of your house or your heart or whatever, but then she thought, "No, it's more than that." She thought of the lines of a song she had written: "Then it came to me that she had to be free./ I couldn't demand of her, only reach out my hand to her./ And I understood that she only could love me freely." That, for her, Claire, got at the idea of what privacy really dealt with—respect for individuality.

There were certain things you learned only after you got more familiar with people, felt Ruby. Like when she had been staying with Natalie and Jo this spring, she had learned how to tell about times when they wanted to be alone together. During those times she tried to be careful about their space. For example, if she needed to go into the bathroom and they were in there talking (because the bathroom in their house was a place where one person took a bath and one or more people talked to them), she needed to ask permission first; whereas if they had just come home from work and were talking in the bathroom, she wouldn't have to do that.

She had always, she felt, been sensitive about this kind of thing. Back in her childhood years, privacy for her had meant a bedroom door she could lock or a space she could call her own in a house, a place where usually, by limiting access from the outside, you gained freedom. It was a place where you could write or sleep or make love by telling people not to come in, by putting a lock on the door or not telling them what you were thinking. There was some kind of feeling about safety that she had when she thought about privacy, her own and that of the community. There was something about manners that affected it. There was also permission-giving going on.

In reality, said Ruth, she would have much preferred that her private life be her private life and that she wouldn't have to talk about it. There were parts of herself she only showed to people who were very close to her. In order to keep something that was very good safe and whole, she felt, you couldn't keep blathering it off to a lot of people. It just wouldn't work.

Privacy for her, said Lisa, was being alone, being alone in her own territory.

It was being alone, said Marla. There was information privacy and being alone.

It was being alone among people, felt Aurora, like a room in a house.

It was a self-indulging aloneness, said Francis.

It was something some people seemed to need more than others, said Leslie. She had always been a person who had to have it and at certain times especially. She might write in her journal then, or listen to music, or spend time on photography. During that time she was thinking and calming down and re-fueling.

There were certain behaviors she would engage in only if she were alone, felt Jill, or only in a situation of unconditional positive regard where people weren't going to judge what they were seeing. She needed the time and the space. She needed the freedom to pursue living the way she wanted to live and not to be subject to anyone else's dictates. That included the people in her peer group and those in her community.

Postscript

A day draws to a close. Helen worries about when her children will get home; Gloria considers her day at work and, again, thoughts cross her mind about telling them at the church that she is a lesbian; Gayle prepares for a meeting at the Women's Shelter and thinks about who she will discuss it with later; Ellen gets ready for a class. Chip and Jessica plan another party at their house. Diana paces her kitchen, troubled that Meg still intends to see Bronwyn, while Meg, in her study, is equally troubled by Diana's lack of understanding of her. Jill takes a long walk to think things over, stopping to wave as Pat drives quietly by in her patrol car in the darkening night.

Martha gets out her bike for the ride over to Mitzi's; Jenny, finished with softball practice, walks alone back to her car, wondering if she will be too tired for work the next morning if she goes to the bar. Alison, already at the bar, is playing pool with several others. Frankie sits quietly at home by herself— Janet has gone out—listening to a Cris Williamson album. Elsewhere, Lilith, too, is listening to the same album, taking very much to heart the lines:

Hurts like the devil not havin' you around.
To wake up in the morning, and be without the sound
Of your breathin' deep and easy, right before my eyes.

> Oh you left too soon and I wonder if you were just a
> nice surprise.*

In time, of course, things change. Gradually Lilith gets over Gayle. Helen eventually leaves town; so do Nell and Judith. Chip and Jessica split up. Marla withdraws from her central role in the community. By a similar token, new people enter; new couples and new alliances form. Yet the community is ongoing. Its problems persist.

When members of this community speak of privacy and of their relationships with one another, they tell us, most importantly perhaps, about struggles over identity. This study has explored some of those struggles and their source in a central internal conflict of the community, the conflict between merger and separation, between joining and remaining apart. Each chapter has presented a different angle of vision on the difficulties individuals face in the community as a result of this conflict and has suggested, as well, how they respond to those difficulties. No one of the chapters or points of view stands alone, but together they form a portrait, and an explanation, of a collective experience.

The Mirror Dance suggests, I think, that individuals come to lesbian communities—as they do to other groups and organizations—with the desire for being accepted as unique individuals as much as for being similar to others. Yet the desire to be accepted as a person who is different from others in a group— or from another in a relationship—is often hidden. It is not spoken of as frequently or as publicly as is the desire for confirmation of a common identity. In addition, it is often accompanied by fears of rejection. Quite frequently, we believe that we are more likely to be loved if we are reflections of others than if we are different; we often tend to experience our difference as a vulnerability; and often, especially if we are women, we have difficulty knowing how to feel comfortable if we are not merged.

In the lesbian community of this study, although the desire for affirmation of a shared identity is extremely strong, so is the quest for individuality. There is a constant tension between fears of loss of a sense of self—as a result of being overwhelmed or abandoned—and the efforts of individuals to strive for personal change and growth. Individuals enter the community and draw back, become involved with each other and pull apart. Their transitions from one time to the next are often painful. They are frequently more vulnerable in their chosen group than in the outside world, and more easily hurt by rejection. Yet they persist in efforts to understand and to overcome, to provide their own world with its own rules and boundaries and its slowly evolving sense of safety.

As the previous chapters indicate, the web of personal entanglements in which identity is formed in this lesbian community, or in any community, is exceedingly complex. *The Mirror Dance* has attempted not to simplify that complexity, as social science ordinarily does, but rather to present it in something like its original form by depicting the community through the voices of its members. The women of this community express contradictory desires for oneness and for separate identity. They struggle together and alone. They speak of experiences particular to lesbians. At the same time, they inform us about problems we all face. Like the women of this study in relation to their group, we are all to some extent outsiders in the communities to which we belong. Yet we need our communities to take us in when we are uncomfortable and ambivalent as much as we need them to welcome us when we seem to fit in, when we merge and conform. There is perhaps no more worthy endeavor in social life than the struggle to build communities that might be truly accepting of their members. This study has recorded that in a midwestern town, in their own way, a small group of women attempted to create such a community.

APPENDIX

Fiction and Social Science*

This appendix argues that we can expand our options for writing up social science field research by using methods of fiction. It examines fiction and social science as alternative approaches to representing reality, both in order to identify difficulties that the use of fiction raises for social science and to suggest the nature of the rewards that fiction offers. In particular, it considers how methods of fiction can add new dimensions to the analysis of organizations and communities.

The discussion is organized in three parts. The first (Grounds for Confusion) compares fiction and social science as approaches to representing reality. The second (The Fiction Temptation in Social Science) looks at social science's characteristically ambivalent stance toward fiction. The third (Patterns of Description) reports on two of the author's studies that were designed to experiment with this ambivalence, and evaluates their results.

*This essay provides a retrospective look at The Mirror Dance in the context of the case study tradition in sociology. It was originally presented as a paper at the Annual Meetings of the American Sociological Association, San Francisco, Sept. 1982. I am indebted to the following people for their help with earlier drafts of this work: Estelle B. Freedman, James G. March, John Sutton, Ann Swidler, and Michal Tamuz.

Appendix

Grounds for Confusion

Fiction and social science are usually seen as very different approaches to representing reality. They have different persuasive rhetorics, they deal differently with evidence, and they offer different kinds of rewards to readers. Yet these approaches also have fundamental similarities. Important among these similarities is the fact that both fiction and social science seek to model the world. Furthermore, they both take the modeling problem seriously, in a way that journalism, for example, does not. This is especially evident when we look at the fiction of novels and compare it with the social science that appears in "case studies" of organizations and communities. Here we find that both fiction and social science seek to weave a pattern of truth, to make what Booth, in speaking of the novel, has described as a structure or shape of events that will seem "a probable reflection of the shapes into which life itself falls" (Booth, 1961: 56). This happens no matter how imaginative the fiction or mundane the social science. There is pattern in each which, to some degree, is reflective, representative, or real.

Historically, Berger has noted, both the modern novel and contemporary social science have common roots in the eighteenth century, a century in which imaginative writers as well as scholars "began in unprecedented proportions and intensity to ask systematically why things happen among and to masses of human beings." During this period, although imaginative writers, or storytellers, still wanted to entertain as they had done in previous centuries, they wanted more than ever before "to offer explanations and guides for behavior," much as did their scholarly counterparts (Berger, 1977: 12).

Nelson, in his study of the dilemma of the Renaissance storyteller (how was the teller of incredible tales, the maker of play and "beast fable" to answer charges of frivolity?), similarly reminds us that although "in practice modern librarians and booksellers rarely find it difficult to separate 'fiction' from 'nonfiction,' " the signs by which they make this distinction are relatively new. These signs reflect the conventional form of the contemporary novel (Nelson, 1973: 38–39). What is more, he points out, as have other scholars, that beneath these signs, beneath the conventional forms, an ambivalence exists about the distinction between fiction and nonfiction that has long troubled both tellers of imaginative tales and those who claim that their tales should pass for true (Nelson, 1973: 38–55; Berger, 1977: 162–185; Roberts, 1972; James, 1957: 259–267; Adam, 1975).

Uncomfortably and perhaps most significantly, this ambivalence is reflected in similarities between approaches found in the most modern of contemporary novels and what may be viewed as the most modern of nonfiction's attempts to come to terms with reality: the strategies of social science. Berger speaks of the tendency of modern novels to downgrade both plot and the importance of character and to reduce the obvious role of the author, an effort which takes the novelist out of the role of omniscient narrator and emphasizes the reality of a world "so complex" that things can be presented "only from various and limited points of view." This, notes Berger, puts the novelist "into close relation with [contemporary] philosophers, if not scientists" (Berger, 1977: 245, 246).

In light of such close relation, what becomes of the distinction between fiction and social science? In theory, at least, that distinction can be summarized as follows: social scientists discover things; novelists invent them. Social scientists develop worlds based on observation. They are concerned about "reality." Novelists make things up. Their realm is that of the "imagination." Social scientists develop and test hypotheses using systematic procedures for handling data or evidence. They seek, through their methods, to minimize the extent to which illusion guides perception. Their wish is to be objective, to be faithful to a world "out there." Novelists, on the other hand, seek to use illusion and deception in the service of their art. Their faithfulness is to an inner world, to the inspired individual vision and to the way that such vision can convey a profound and lasting sense of truth. This is the difference in its most stark form. The problem, however, is that when not considered starkly, the difference fades. We find that, in practice, social scientists often do what novelists do: they invent, they use illusion and inner vision, they focus on the unique and the particular (e.g., Geertz, 1973). Novelists, similarly, are often discoverers, testing ideas against evidence, developing generalizations, and seeking to be faithful to details of external experience (e.g., Bryant, 1978). Such overlap between the two genres is uncomfortable. It suggests a potential confusion of boundaries—a confusion between the imagined and the real, between moral lesson and reflection of fact.

Not surprisingly, in the face of such confusion, we find that on both sides of the line between fiction and social science, there is a tendency to emphasize distinctions. We find novelists, for example, arguing in the extreme that their fictions bear no resemblance to reality and that any such notion will undermine their success in creating those elaborate structures of deception through which their vision of the truth may be grasped (Calderwood and Toliver, 1968: 55–70, 73–83). We find among social scientists, on the other hand, a view of fiction as potentially threatening to social science's distinctive task, since fiction seems clearly not concerned with systematic procedures and tests of validity—in effect with the kind of accountability—that the models of social science require. For the social scientist, fiction is a temptation which repeatedly must be refused.*

---

*The presence of *literary forms* within social science has been acknowledged in several recent works, however. See, for example, Gusfield (1976) and Manning (1979). White (1973) provides a discussion of literary forms in history that is also relevant to the social sciences. Sanday (1979) presents a useful discussion of the distinction between making a fiction or a science that extends suggestions of Geertz (1973). Although the fiction temptation is often refused in social science, there are exceptional works that embrace it. See, for example, Bluebond-Langner (1978).

How much of the rejection of fiction that occurs in social science is necessary for boundary clarification and how much is an attempt to escape problems that really are as central to social science as they are to fiction, and that arise across a broad range of works and recur over time? What would happen if we were not to reject, but instead to talk about how we might more fully acknowledge and work with the ambiguity of the fiction/social science distinction within social science? Some answers are suggested by considering how fiction already figures in our studies, the problems it raises, and the way that these problems have been dealt with.

The Fiction Temptation in Social Science

One of the studies that tells us most about fiction in social science is William F. Whyte's *Street Corner Society* (1943). In his Preface to *Street Corner Society*, Whyte notes that "fictitious names are given to all characters in this book" (p. ix). The suggestion is clear: there is fantasy at work here. Names are inventions and the people of real life have become "characters" in Whyte's work, agents in a hypothetical drama whose reality is *Street Corner Society*, not life independent of it. In his Introduction, Whyte goes on to encourage us to become immersed in a fictitious world. He begins by setting the scene, "In the heart of 'Eastern City' . . ." (p. xvii). He then proceeds to tell us that if we can get to know some of the people of this city "intimately," then we can learn something important. If we can understand "the relationships between little guy and big guy, big shot and little guy, and big shot and big shot, then we [will] know how Cornerville society is organized" (p. xxii). The fiction, in other words, will pay off.

Yet Whyte also expresses uncertainty about his fictional device. In the very next chapter (Chapter I: "Doc and His Boys"), after painting an initial picture of the Cornerville group and its interrelationships, he cautions, "If this were a work of fiction, the story would now be finished" (p. 42). The story continues, however, as Whyte, relying primarily on descriptions of inter-personal events and subgroup context, "explains" the social structure of Cornerville and of racketeering activities he has found there.

In a long and revealing Appendix to *Street Corner Society*, Whyte tells us about his method for constructing this explana-tion. The construction of *Street Corner Society*, he notes, is based on his having come to see a "pattern" in his data. This pattern is "not purely an artistic creation," however; it is not a piece of fiction. It "represents the life we are observing"—the life he had observed during his several years of fieldwork and participant observation (p. 280). What is more, he advises, this pattern is a result not only of initial recognition but of testing: "Once we think we see it, we must reexamine our notes and perhaps set out to gather new data in order to determine whether the pattern *adequately* represents the life we are observing" or whether it is "*simply* a product of our imagination" (p. 280, italics mine).

Whyte further explains that the pattern he used did not become clear to him until he began to write up his data. At that point, he realized he was not writing a sociological study "in the usual sense of that term." He was not doing what had been done in *Middletown*, for instance: "The reader who examines *Middle-town* will note that it is written about people in general in that community. Individuals or groups do not figure in the story except as they illustrate points that the authors are making" (p. 322).

In his own study, however, Whyte was very conscious that rather than looking at "the general characteristics of classes of people," he was looking at "Doc, Chic, Tony Cataldo, George Ravello and others." Instead of getting a cross-sectional picture of the community at a particular point in time," he was "dealing with a time sequence of interpersonal events." He was "building up the structure and functioning of the community through intensive examination of some of its parts" (pp. 357–358). In relating these parts together, he was, in sum, "seeking to build a sociology based on observed interpersonal events." That, for him, was "the chief methodological and theoretical meaning of *Street Corner Society*" (p. 358).

This last statement concludes Whyte's Appendix and it is a strong and potentially troublesome statement for social science. It says that Whyte's description of "particular people, situations, and events" in a hypothetical yet to some extent representative Cornerville is both his method and his theory. Implied is that in reading Whyte's description, in following the way he uses "stories" of individuals and groups (p. 357), we are learning not only about those individuals but about the social structure of which they are part. Whyte's stories, in other words, create his theory and are not just evidence for it. We understand his explanation of racketeering and, more basically, his theory of social organization, not because we are told its tenets in abstract or "theoretical" terms (although we are told some of it in these terms in the end), but because we are led through a world in which we can develop an experiential sense of the way that individual actions relate to each other and to a larger whole.

In *Street Corner Society*, Whyte thus reminds us that it is not theoretical language that builds theory but the recognition of patterns of interrelationship. These patterns can be represented in highly concrete and particular terms: in the way that Lou Danaro and Fred Mackey continue as members, but become critical, after Doc deliberately misses three meetings and drops out of the Italian Community Club, for instance (p. 71); in the report that "Tony was to pay the rent and light bills in return for running card games and taking bets on the dog races" one summer, and that "when Carlo heard of this agreement, he once again called the boys a 'bunch of dirty double-crossers'" (p. 152). The *specificity* of such terms, and their related *suggestiveness*, make Whyte's sociology. They enable it effectively to produce a world which is explanation for itself. Yet this success, in turn, raises two crucial problems for social science. These are the problems to which Whyte's repeated concern for distinguishing his work from fiction seem to allude.

The first of these problems is that specificity—making a world seem compelling, actual, rich, as if made of fact—may obscure the knowledge that the reality conveyed by a study, no matter how coherent or compelling, is a fiction. It is an interpretation. This problem, in brief, is that in a study such as Whyte's, we may have difficulty separating out evidence from interpretation. We may not be able to see a world "out there" separate from the study's depiction. The second problem, which is the inverse of the first, is that we may also have difficulty separating such a study's interpretation from its evidence. The study's specificity may blur or even seem to bury the work's fictional structure, making its assumptions and organizing principles unclear.

Together these twin problems—that of specificity producing a world which seems too real (so that we have difficulty separating "evidence" from interpretation), and that of theory becoming embedded in a particular structure of events (so that we can't separate "interpretation" from evidence)—seem threatening to social science, since social science, at least ideally, is committed to the explicit articulation of assumptions and to the separation of data from theory. Social science does not rest easy with theory that is inextricably intertwined with the forms of everyday life.

Thus an orientation such as Whyte's—which suggests that to structure a description is to build an explanation—is somewhat disturbing. In this kind of orientation, the line between science and art, social science and the novel, seems to fade too easily. The social scientist then asserts either that his or her work is not fiction (that other kind of less responsible shaping of events with which it may be confused), or that the events it describes can be better, more adequately, or more fully explained in another way, usually in more abstract terms. Whyte makes both these kinds of assertions in *Street Corner Society*, as perhaps he must. Repeatedly, he reminds us that his description is created, not from whole cloth, but from extensive observation and self-conscious theory. He reassures us, in other words, that his fiction is safe. It does not lead us beyond sociology.

Another case that tells us much about the ambivalence characteristic of social science's response to the temptation of fiction is Warner and Lunt's original Yankee City study, *The Social Life of a Modern Community* (1941). Chapter VII of that study ("Profiles from Yankee City") is a deliberate experiment with fiction followed by a consideration of the contribution of fictional technique to sociological understanding in the Yankee City case. In introducing this chapter, Warner and Lunt tell us that they soon will be describing particular persons, institutions, and incidents, some of which are "composite drawings" and some of which are "entirely imaginary," in order to give us a sense of "the essential social reality" of Yankee City (p. 127). This they acknowledge to be a sense that other measures used in their analysis fail to convey. They then present a series of fourteen vignette-type depictions of local people and their dramas beginning with the following:

> On that Autumn evening Mrs. Henry Adams Brecken-
> ridge was sitting in a large wing chair by the fireplace
> whose dying embers occasionally flared and lighted her
> pale face and white hair. Behind her, numerous used
> tea cups were scattered on the table. Of her fifty-odd
> guests all but two had departed . . . (p. 128).

The suggestive power of this opening passage is strong. It seems almost an invitation to a mystery. Yet in the end, in the conclusion to their fiction chapter, Warner and Lunt turn away from such specific and evocative phrases, which, they have already told us, they are presenting only as "examples," not, as in Whyte's case, building blocks to a sociology. In their conclusion, after the sixty-eight pages of highly concrete and unembellished description that form the core of their fiction chapter (pp. 128–196), Warner and Lunt seek to speak to us in quite another way. The descriptive material in their chapter needs little analysis, they say. Yet they will summarize "the more general and obvious points": that the first fictional section of their chapter "describes the members of the three upper classes [of Yankee City] in primary interaction" (p. 196), for example; that the seventh and eighth sections, with their "contrasting stories" of Mrs. Wentworth and Mrs. Teppington, show how "successful mobility into the upper classes" may or may not be achieved (p. 197); that the ninth section further illustrates the problem of how "a very small number of upper-class people can control [a] larger number from the lower ranks" (p. 198).

Thus, despite their use of fictional techniques, Warner and Lunt indicate that they are torn between the evocative style that their fictions represent and more explicit analysis. In concluding their fiction chapter, they comment on both approaches. Their analytic summaries are "manifestly inadequate," they caution. The social structure of Yankee City is "too complex to be described with such simple generalities." The composite life histories, social dramas, and depictions of personal behavior that their descriptive, or fictional, passages contain are also inadequate, they say. These passages present a picture that, too, is oversimplified and, in addition, is partial and "subject to the unconscious biases of the writer." Given these inadequacies, Warner and Lunt's solution is to turn to quantitative analysis, which they view as "more adequate" and which they expect will give them a more specific and complete representation of how the different social ranks of Yankee City behave (pp. 200–201).

We may, of course, question the standards that Warner and Lunt use in making this decision, but what is important, for the moment, is not the argument between quantitative and qualitative, or even the argument between general and particular. Rather it is the fact that a fiction of the sort resembling what we find in novels was entertained in the Yankee City analysis. It seemed to offer something that other techniques or approaches lacked. Then, however, it was discarded, or at least considered inappropriate for generating social scientific knowledge.

In more recent studies, too, we find experiments with fiction followed by rejection of such experiments as unsuitable or inadequate for social science. Cavan, in an introduction to her study, "Hippies of the Redwood Forest," has described reasons for such rejection with unusual candor (1971). Like Whyte, Cavan reports on the moment when she turned from her fieldwork to writing up her data. She was, at that point, though still in the field, ready to write up events she had observed in her previous months of research. Yet she "could not come to 'sociological terms' with them." The result of her first effort was "a 30 page epic saga" titled "Dia of Jax." It "described life in a barbaric village in some mythic empire." As far as Cavan could see, she was not "'doing sociology'" (p. 11).

In search of a solution, Cavan reports that she looked forward to the return of her research associate to their field site, "hoping that the presence of another sociologist would help clarify my perspective of what 'doing sociology' entailed and that I would stop writing mythic sagas, and start writing more systematic, objective accounts" (p. 11). Finally, as both Cavan's study itself and her personal account of it tell us, she began to concentrate more conventionally on "the methodological problem of 'describing social structure'" (p. 12). She started developing "categories" for analyzing her data and from this formed the final contours of her study. In the process, however, Cavan notes that the uniqueness of the events she had originally observed in the field began to blur; their exotic features faded. She "no longer saw the settlement at Jax as a barbarian village in a mythic empire. Rather, it became like Veterans housing at UCLA." Thus, in the process of ordering her data, she killed her exhilaration. The community—the hypothetical community of Jax—became "a commonplace scene" and what was left was "another job to finish" (p. 15).

Cavan's experience, like that of Warner and Lunt, and Whyte, begins to suggest, I think, that the novelist's fiction is curiously troublesome in social science. Our studies display an ambivalence toward it that does not seem to go away. Although methods of fiction beckon and although they may allow us, as social scientists, to present a much needed feel for life, they also often seem to threaten to take us off course, to involve us in that "other business" which does not, in the terms we know, reflect a concern for faithfulness to data and a commitment to the development of theory.

Yet if, as Marianne Moore has said of poetry, it (poetry) presents "for inspection imaginary gardens with real toads in them" (Calderwood and Toliver, 1968: 74), and something not too different can be said of social science, it may be about time that we more fully acknowledge the novelist's or poet's fiction in our midst for what it truly is. We already admit imaginative reconstructions in social science if they are called hypotheses and if the claim is made that they are testable. But what if the hypothesis is itself made up of detailed, concrete observations? What if it looks like Cornerville, a mythic saga, or a long prose poem? What if it is made of human beings, their homes, their meanings, their dialogues, their scenes, the chaos of their self-reflections, the evocative specificity of their lives? We have such studies, many of them, the whole qualitative case study tradition based heavily on field research that is much indebted to Whyte.

But because we are defensive about writing fiction, we often avoid speaking of a central logic that these studies follow, which appears in much quantitative work as well, and which, however "non-scientific," is integral to social science. Whyte, in Street Corner Society, made an important assertion with his statement that his method of description was his theory (1943: 358). Such an assertion raises problems for social science. These are problems, however, that disclaimers that a work is not fiction, or explanations of a work's main points, do not solve. This is because the fundamental problem that fiction brings to social science, or perhaps more accurately, keeps alive in social science, is the problem of choice in structuring description. Acknowledgement of fiction opens up this problem like a can of worms. It causes us to ask, exactly what are the choices available to us? What are our limits? What are the logics or rationales for making one choice rather than another?

How much imagination should we allow in our studies, for example? How much detail and of what kind? How much implicit character? What should we do with poetic suggestiveness? What kinds of narrative structures should we use? What, in fact, do these terms mean in a work of social science? How much control can we actually have? Such questions take us into a different language for talking about our models of reality than standard social science methodology provides. Yet it is perhaps a language we need to develop.

In sum, then, in discussing the works of Whyte, Warner and Lunt, and Cavan noted previously, I have sought to indicate the presence of the novelist's type of fiction within social science, to point to a discomfort social scientists feel when faced with this presence, and to suggest how social scientists typically respond to the temptation that fiction represents. Although the three studies cited are each unique in their specific solutions to the problems that fiction raises for social science, the attitudes and responses that these studies illustrate can be found in a broad range of studies. Repeatedly, we may note that fiction is referred to and that it is disclaimed, discarded, and employed, often all in the same work. Fiction in social science is viewed as a temptation whose central danger is the freedom of imagination it suggests (i.e., novelists "make things up," while social scientists cannot). Yet as a temptation, fiction also offers important rewards. It promises the possibility of imbuing the models of social science with a much needed "truth to life." It offers a major alternative for developing the creative and inventive possibilities of social science and for extending our abilities to produce valid models. The attempt to rid ourselves of fiction because of the problems it raises is an attempt to rid ourselves of a vital and healthy exploration.

Yet while wholesale rejection of fiction may be neither possible nor desirable, social science's stance of ambivalence

185

toward fiction may be fruitful. For it is precisely in the jockeying back and forth between ideals of imagination and accountability, implication and plain-speaking, that social science comes into being and fashions and solves its particular problems. This is no less true when the jockeying includes an element of imagination that resembles that of the novelist than it is when the imagination is more fully tailored to resemble that of the physicist. There are many possible resolutions of the social scientific ambivalence toward fiction. My argument here is not for any one resolution, but for an extension of our ability to talk about them all.

In the concluding section of this paper, I want to discuss two studies of my own in order to corroborate some of the points made earlier and to suggest directions for new work. These were two studies that were deliberately designed to experiment with methods of fiction in the sociological case study tradition.

Patterns of Description

Hip Capitalism: A Basic Approach

The first study concerned the cooptation of an underground radio station (Krieger, 1979a). In that study, I sought to explain how a hippy rock radio station in San Francisco "sold out" to become part of a larger, more conservative "establishment." My study was based on a year of in-depth interviewing with approximately ninety people involved with the station and on the collection of documentary evidence. At the end of my research year as I turned to writing up my data, like Cavan and Whyte, I found that I was drawn toward something resembling fiction.

I wanted to explain the cooptation process the station had experienced by describing that process in its own terms rather than by talking about it in abstract or summary terms. My desire, in other words, was to develop an approach in which the details or evidence of my case would tell my story for me, a story of how the radio station went from idealistic origins and independent ownership in 1967 to corporate ownership and commercial success by 1972. I felt that this shift could be explained best by "showing" rather than "telling" about how subtle changes in the station's organizational routine were linked to more dramatic incidents and these to changes in individual and corporate ideology.*

I therefore decided on a form I later came to call a multiple-person stream of consciousness narrative (Krieger, 1979b). This was perhaps in part because I was reading Virginia Woolf's *The Years* at the time, a novel in which the internal dramas of individuals are combined to form an inter-generational family saga that continues over many years. My own narrative in the radio station case was composed of the voices, stories, and self-reflections of the different people I had interviewed and the written reports I had read. These were joined together to form a composite story of what the radio station's cooptation had been like, and of how, and implicitly why, that process had occurred.

In constructing this composite story, I considered myself to be very much a social scientist in that I was committed to developing an explanation and to being systematic in moving from my data to my interpretation, from the details of my case to a structure for explaining them. I deliberately devised and followed rules for doing this. Two of these rules were central. The first was that I had to construct my account almost entirely by paraphrasing from my interview and documentary evidence. According to this rule, I would allow myself no analytic or theoretical commentary in the body of my text. My evidence, faithfully interpreted, would have to do this work for me. My only commentary would be in the structure of the description I evolved to move from one paraphrased passage to the next in order to form a larger narrative whole.

My second principal rule, then, had to do with key assumptions of that larger whole, the implicit theory of my

*For a pertinent discussion of the distinction between showing and telling, see Booth (1961: 3–20).

study. This rule was that my account should not be partial to any one person or point of view, or view any one kind of change in the station's environment as more important than any other. Rather it would have a primary commitment to making plain a pattern of detail in which everything was important. This emphasis on pattern of detail rather than on a particular angle of vision, line of interpretation, or single theory was consistent, I felt, with pattern modeling as articulated by Kaplan. "We know the reason for something," Kaplan notes, "either when we can fit it into a known pattern, or else when we can deduce it from other known truths." In a pattern model, as different from a deductive model, "something is explained when it is so related to a set of other elements that together they constitute a unified system." An event, whether "fact" or "law," is understood "by identifying it as a specific part in an organized whole" (Kaplan, 1964: 327–335; see also Diesing, 1971: 160–167).

Thinking in terms of a pattern model and following my rules for evidence and interpretation, I produced a systematically structured description in the radio station case. This description concerned the collective or organizational experience of cooptation. My account was written so as to guide a reader through the station's cooptation process so that the reader could then draw her or his own interpretive conclusions about why it occurred. While I did not explicitly tell my readers what to think, I did implicitly assert my own explanation as one possible alternative by structuring the situation I described at its most basic level: deciding what to admit as evidence, setting up linkages, manipulating detail, piecing together the story of the station's cooptation as it seemed to me to make sense, or to be explicable.

Now all this seemed reasonable but it took me far from a conventional social science model in which theory is separable from data and a reader is told in general terms how a thing described is to be explained. My approach made me feel more like a novelist in that I was constructing a world, and conveying my message, by weaving a pattern that was, by and large, a suggestive scaffolding, an illusion built of the concrete and the actual: the furniture in the station, the names of records, the rates salesmen used for selling time. It centered on feelings one person had for another and especially for Tom Donahue, the "Big Daddy" of the station, who weighed 400 pounds and used to be in Top-40 and who liked to recall the time back in the beginning when they met the payroll at KMPX with "muddy money": $1,000 in small bills on loan from a dope dealer friend of the station's top salesman who had to dig them up from where he had them buried in his yard, so the bills had caked mud on them when they were distributed to the staff.

The account focused on such experiences as how coming to work in 1970 was different than it had been in 1969, though nobody could agree on why; on how a man like Thom O'Hair, the "Montana Banana," finally became the station's program director and was militaristic in his execution of that role, after Paul Boucher, his predecessor, "flaked out" and drifted into Scientology; and on the way that the army at last gave permission for Doug Dunlop, a salesman who had been with the station since it was classical and who had once tried out for the boy lead in *Lassie*, to wear sideburns and slightly longer hair. Such things were noted and the pattern of transition they strongly suggested was repeatedly affirmed. That pattern, however, was never explicitly theoretically summarized (Krieger, 1979a).

Although I felt that I remained a social scientist in taking this approach to case construction in my study (my pattern of detail, after all, could be tested against further evidence; it was generalizable to other situations that might be seen as similar; I could *really* have written a novel if that was what I had wanted), a persistent sense of falling between the lines left me uncomfortable. Often, especially late at night, my work seemed to me to be neither fiction *nor* social science. The closest match in form for it that I could find was in the "new journalism," but I didn't feel particularly good about that. When several years later I undertook another study, I had in mind trying to be more conventional as a social scientist, thereby avoiding feeling troubled further about the nature and legitimacy of my work.

The Mirror Dance: Exacerbating the Discomfort

My second study dealt with problems of individuality in a midwestern women's community, a lesbian group in which, I felt, such problems took particularly interesting form. In this study, I sought to explain how a loss of individuality, or a loss of sense of self, occurs in a social group. I wanted to show how threats to an individual's sense of personal boundaries might be a result of patterns of subgroup culture and sociability and of a subgroup's relationship to its outside world (Krieger, 1983). My study was based on a year of participant-observation culminating in two months of intensive interviewing with seventy-eight community members and associates. When I turned to writing up my results, I at first tried an approach which used my interview data as examples of more general theoretical points. This was in order to avoid the discomfort about legitimacy that I had felt in my radio station study. I also experimented with a subjective, first-person account, since I had been a community member and I thought I might use my experience as a probe of the community environment.

Ultimately, I put both these efforts aside, however, and opted for a modified version of the radio station method. I did this not in imitation of my first study, but because it seemed to offer a solution to problems of the second case as well. It seemed to evolve out of my desire, on the one hand, to write a novel about the community's social intrigues and its sense of being a haven or home in its midwestern small-town setting, and, on the other, out of a desire to diagnose objectively, or in collective terms, some of the problems of the community. In my final attempt to write up my study, then, I found myself using the same two basic rules I had used in the radio station case: the rule of faithfulness to evidence and the rule of constructing a composite account that would set forth a pattern of detail in relation to which the problem I was concerned about—loss of sense of self—might be understood.

The main difference between this second case and the first, however, was that in this new study, I attempted to be even more strict in my method than I had been before. I paraphrased my data even more closely and used my interview notes as the only source for writing up my account. These were changes which, I should note, did not mean less interpretive work on my part than the radio station study had required, but, in fact, more. In structuring my description from my notes, I took even fewer imaginative liberties than I had in the radio station case. I added very little of my own wording to my text beyond crediting paraphrased passages to different speakers and identifying when speakers changed. I therefore became almost absent as a narrator. I was "painting a picture" this time, and a modern abstract one at that, rather than "telling a story" as I had done before. My desire was to have the voices and language of the women I had interviewed provide their own systematic self-reflection, to have them suggest, in their own terms, the form of a pattern that might explain the problems of individuality the community posed for its members. I could orchestrate these women's voices, with all the care for a faithful grasp of their situation and its meanings that I could manage, but my rule was that I should do little more.

The result of this more strict approach was that my depiction in *The Mirror Dance* turned out to be quite austere. It consisted solely of the voices of the community with minimal transition between them and no generally integrative narrative voice. The austerity of this pattern pleased me. I felt that my study was all the more valid because of it. I also felt that this second analysis was better than my first. It was more sophisticated, more subtle, and more clearly sociological than the radio station study had been, and also more complex in its suggestive power. Its detail was probably more accurate; its structure was more novelistically inventive.

Appendix

The study conveyed the central excitement of a community's gossip, of everybody talking about themselves and each other, who was going with whom, and why. It allowed a reader to follow "the hotline that went around all the time" in the community, to know the community from its center to its margins, to go to parties, visit bars, share in the breakups of couples, the raising of children, become immersed in the many internal dialogues and private social and sexual entanglements that knit the community together, to hear opinions about community leaders and norms that, because these opinions might be critical or sensitive, were not widely shared. It provided, in other words, a kind of bird's-eye view of one distinct sphere of social activity, a kind of view that in actual life is often unobtainable even though it is "what everybody knows," but that in fiction and social science can be offered as a gift. This was what I felt I had done in *The Mirror Dance.*

I was therefore surprised that many of the readers of this study reported that they experienced discomfort with it. The critical comments of these readers were mainly of two types. First, and most important, was a discomfort with my method. Readers experiencing this discomfort felt that I had simply presented what people had said, that I had done "mere description," or a mere presentation of data. They would have appreciated an authorial voice: either a traditional social scientific voice doing analytic or theoretical commentary throughout the body of the work and explicitly tying it together, or a traditional novelistic or literary voice that would have carried them along with a more eloquent narrative style than I had been willing to use. In the best of all possible worlds, such readers, I imagined, would have preferred both types of voices.

Secondly, some readers reported having difficulty with what seemed to be an ambivalence in my sympathies that showed in the account. My readers, I soon found, wanted very much to feel good about the community of my study, to like the individual people in it, and to come away with a sense that the community and its members were triumphing over their problems. These readers felt disturbed and saddened when this was not possible, when I emphasized the difficulties, confusions, and painfulness of the struggles for individuality in the community, for example, as I did throughout the study, although more so in some chapters than in others. Readers experiencing discomfort with my sympathies, or, perhaps more accurately, with the overall "feeling sense" of my account, reported not knowing whether to be angry and dissatisfied with me about this discomfort, because of biases in my style of depiction, or to be angry and dissatisfied with my characters because of how they behaved. These characters, for example, too easily or too often, seemed to compromise their ideals, or to have unrealistic expectations of themselves and each other.

These two kinds of discomfort—with my method and with the apparent sympathies of my account—bothered me a good deal. Not only did they catch me by surprise since I had expected that I had done better in this second case, but they also touched on sore points, areas in which I had hoped not to fail but to succeed impressively. I had wanted my narrative structure to be accepted and appreciated for all the interpretive and compositional art that went into it. I valued being sympathetic to my characters and I wanted my account to reflect that. In addition, I did not want my "sociology" to be at the expense of my community. I wanted it, on the contrary, to contribute to the self-understanding of that community by enabling the community to see why its problems were difficult and to appreciate its own solutions to them.

It took me some time, therefore, before I could begin to see that the discomforts my readers reported might be interpreted as evidence of my study's success as well as of its failure. They were evidence of its success with its own kind of task. First, I had been so faithful to my data that the hypothetical in my study was mistaken for the real. My particular structuring of the case was felt to be so true that it seemed that I had done no structuring at all, or no structuring that, in any important sense, altered my data. Second, the absence of a narrative or analytic voice was, paradoxically, a presence, one whose main effect was to call attention to my study's device: its pattern for structuring evidence. This somewhat uncomfortable device was necessary to the kind of social science I was making, for I did not want my work to be smooth in style. It had to convey the disjointed feel of multiple voices and a contradictory social setting. Were the work more comfortable, it would have been dishonest. Similarly, the account could not be entirely sympathetic. I was not able to speak with unambivalent feelings or without a sense of frustration. This was true whether readers, myself included, liked it or not.

What I could do, however, and had done, was to fashion a whole that was smooth enough and sufficiently reassuring so that it would entice and guide the reader. My strategy was to create a tempting semblance of the familiar: a sense of expected linkages, likeable people, and a positively valued social setting, only then to jar that sense by structuring another kind of description, one that took form not because it was comfortable or conventional, but because of what it was capable of showing about the nature of the problem I wanted to explain. A journalist could write comfortable or conventional description, I thought; so could a novelist or a historian, if she or he so chose; but a social scientist such as I could not. My social scientist would write an ambiguous and disconcerting descriptive account which would alternately frustrate and reward its readers by playing with the reader's expectations about fiction and social science.

On the one hand, I would fail to satisfy the reader by the form of my invention as a traditional novelist might; on the other, I would fail to satisfy with a free-standing theoretical explanation as might a conventional social scientist. I would tempt my reader to expect both the pleasures of imagination and of accountability and repeatedly stop short of providing them. I would offer neither felicities of style nor simplicities of generalization. What my studies would do, instead, was to provide a kind of bumpy buggy ride through the back roads of one or another group's collective internal consciousness, and this in explanation of a central problem or process of their situation. No wonder readers expressed discomfort!

My radio station study, *Hip Capitalism*, was less disturbing than *The Mirror Dance*. I think this was because it was more conventional. It was modeled, to a greater degree, after a storytelling form called "history." Yet *The Mirror Dance* was the direction in which I wanted to go, and in which I wish to keep going. I want to learn to invent more and to suggest more within social science so that my accounts can say something about possibilities for representation as well as about the nature of the real world.

Conclusion

My argument is not for my version of doing social science or for my own way of merging fiction and social science. My approach clearly has its difficulties. Its chief advantage, I think, is its faithfulness to an interpretive whole that constructs reality in a way that neither raw data nor abstractions can provide. A case in my method becomes a model. This model, although it is fashioned from multiple viewpoints, enables an unusually high degree of insight into the totality of a collective experience. The disadvantages of the method are that it places conflicting demands upon a reader. The reader has to work to benefit from an explanation that, while self-evident, is not obvious. As in a novel, this explanation is understood largely through experience rather than through an intellectual process. Yet the experience of a case can be analyzed. Its explanation can be tested against further evidence. Its pattern can be extended to see if additional data fit. For purposes of analysis and testing, a reader's discomfort in response to a study can be used as a guide.

One case can generalize to another in this method as a result of similar processes that are primarily experiential. This occurs when a reader comes to feel or see characteristics of the first or model case in a second. To the extent that the first case is

Appendix

internally accurate, rich and complex, and guided by a strong underlying vision, it will enable better generalization to other cases, since it will provide more memorable points of recognition and comparison. It will offer more standards of reference for telling likeness from difference, for matching the processes or characteristics of one situation appropriately with those of another. Finally, to the extent that a model case takes issue with conventional modes of description and wages its own internal battle with them, it will offer us fresh insights and new theoretical ideas.

This, I think, is the method's appeal for me. I am basically concerned that the worlds we describe in social science too often reflect a limited set of currently fashionable theoretical views. We tell the same stories over and over; we paint the same pictures. We don't let in very many dimensions of the outside world. Although our methods are designed to prevent this, what happens most often is not that our arguments follow from our evidence, but just the reverse. Our models are not only abstract, but also out of touch. I think that descriptive explanations, with their primary faithfulness to data and detail, are one way to break out of this pattern, to show more of what is "really" going on. They require a combination of the novelist's and the social scientist's mind: a willingness to construct a representation as a novelist might, yet at the same time a desire to think like a social scientist. They do not require giving up the social scientist's purposes but they do require opening up the forms in which the social scientist usually goes about pursuing these purposes. They require a willingness to try new things.

Someone once said to me that a social scientist experimenting with fiction could at best make third-rate novels. I don't think such people make novels at all, to come down clearly on one side of the fiction/social science ambivalence. At least this has been so in my own case.

I do think that it is worth remembering, however, that what lasts from most of the best field-based studies we have in sociology, the classics like *Middletown, Street Corner Society, The*

Levittowners, or *Talley's Corner,* is much more than can be comprehended in the abstractions that are drawn from any case by the author at the time of writing. Rather what lasts, after many years, and perhaps most significantly, is a more pervasive, amorphous, and deeply informative *sense of the case itself,* a sense of the structure of reality it presents with its description, at whatever level of abstraction or specificity that description is made. This is very important. I think that it takes both the novelist's and the social scientist's kind of imagination to make such cases. It also takes both kinds of imagination on the part of the reader to appreciate them, to realize the kinds of problems these cases must deal with and resolve.

Those problems, as I have sought to indicate in each section of this paper, are not minor. What is more, they recur, in some form, in all our modeling efforts in social science. Our persuasive success always depends, in part, on our poetic suggestiveness, on our acumen in making a particular pattern of detail evoke a broader "truth to life." It has been my purpose in this paper to argue for a more full acknowledgment and discussion of the novelist's fiction in social science, especially in those qualitative field-based studies where it is most prominent. I feel that such discussion can help us produce better, more imaginative, and more valid work. In the end, I think, the scatter of the tea cups of *Yankee City* provides a valuable lesson, as does the unused mythic saga of Jax, and the discomfort that such inquiries as mine may raise. That is, that the alternative of exploring the "softer" side of social science may be well worth the risk.

References

Adam, Ian, ed.
    1975   *This Particular Web: Essays on Middlemarch.* Toronto: University of Toronto Press.
Berger, Morroe
    1977   *Real and Imagined Worlds: The Novel and Social Science.* Cambridge: Harvard University Press.

Appendix

Bluebond-Langner, Myra
 1978 *The Private Worlds of Dying Children.* Princeton: Princeton University Press.
Booth, Wayne C.
 1961 *The Rhetoric of Fiction.* Chicago: University of Chicago Press.
Bryant, Dorothy
 1978 *Writing a Novel.* Berkeley: Ata Books.
Calderwood, James, and Harold Toliver, eds.
 1968 *Perspectives on Fiction.* New York: Oxford University Press.
Cavan, Sherri
 1971 "Hippies of the Redwood Forest." Unpublished manuscript, Department of Sociology, San Francisco State University.
Diesing, Paul
 1971 *Patterns of Discovery in the Social Sciences.* Chicago: Aldine-Atherton.
Geertz, Clifford
 1973 *The Interpretation of Cultures: Selected Essays.* New York: Basic Books.
Gusfield, Joseph
 1976 "The Literary Rhetoric of Science: Comedy and Pathos in Drinking Driver Research." *American Sociological Review,* 41: 16–34.
James, Henry
 1957 *The House of Fiction: Essays on the Novel.* London: Rupert Hart-Davis.
Kaplan, Abraham
 1964 *The Conduct of Inquiry: Methodology for Behavioral Science.* Scranton: Chandler.
Krieger, Susan
 1979a *Hip Capitalism.* Beverly Hills: Sage.
 1979b "Research and the Construction of a Text." *Studies in Symbolic Interaction,* 2: 167–187.
 1983 *The Mirror Dance: Identity in a Women's Community.* Philadelphia: Temple University Press.
Manning, Peter K.
 1979 "Metaphors of the Field: Varieties of Organizational

Discourse." *Administrative Science Quarterly,*
24: 660–671.

Nelson, William
1973   *Fact or Fiction: The Dilemma of the Renaissance
Storyteller.* Cambridge: Harvard University Press.

Roberts, Thomas J.
1972   *When Is Something Fiction?* Carbondale: Southern
Illinois University Press.

Sanday, Peggy Reeves
1979   "The Ethnographic Paradigm(s)." *Administrative
Science Quarterly,* 24: 527–538.

Warner, W. Lloyd, and Paul Lunt
1941   *The Social Life of a Modern Community.* New Haven:
Yale University Press.

White, Hayden
1973   *Metahistory: The Historical Imagination in 19th Century
Europe.* Baltimore: Johns Hopkins University Press.

Whyte, William Foote
1943   *Street Corner Society: The Social Structure of an Italian
Slum.* Chicago: University of Chicago Press.